I ts abundant delights might lead one to imagine himself in heaven. It is between a lake of fresh, very clear water and a river. Canals run through every quarter of the city . . . . The number of bridges have arches so high that vessels with masts can pass under them, and the slope is so well-graded that carts and horses can pass over them. On the lake are numbers of boats and barges for parties of pleasure . . . . A party can enjoy the view of the city with its numberless palaces, temples, monasteries, and gardens full of lofty trees, sloping to the shore.

Marco Polo describing the great city of Hangchow
in the thirteenth century.

INDIA: One of India's great leaders, Akbar (above), flanked by his son (right) and grandson. Vishnu, one of the trinity of Hindu gods, slays an evil spirit who is poisoning the river (top right). Musician and dancer (right) from a 17th-century tapestry.

CHINA: Pots like this miniature (left) were used 3000 years ago to cook over fires. In this Ming dynasty family portrait (top left), the household head is surrounded by his sons and their wives, and his wife and mother. Women iron silk (top) using glowing coals. Fantastic rocks in this landscape suggest the spiritual quality of nature.

9

THE AMERICAS BEFORE COLUMBUS: In an Aztec wedding (above), there was much feasting and praying before the couple "tied the knot" (top center). Statue of a warrior (left) was made by an early people of Peru. They were followed by the Incas, who built the city of Machu Picchu high in the Andes Mountains (right).

AFRICA: Today Benin is a small city in Nigeria, but 500 years ago it was an important capital. Benin's artists created the mask (left) to honor their king. Figures at the top represent the Portuguese who traded with Benin and who were believed to hold great magic. Artists designed the metal court musician (left) and bronze and ivory leopard, a symbol of the power of Benin's king (below).

13

BYZANTINE AND MUSLIM EMPIRES: The emperor of
the Byzantine empire (left) was also head of the Christian
church. The second great empire centered in the Middle
East was the Muslim. In the western corner of its empire
in Spain, Muslims built the Alhambra palace (above).

PART
1

INDIA

Look at the world map on page 214 and you'll see a triangle of land sticking out at the bottom of Asia. This is the Indian subcontinent.

It doesn't look very big—just a bump on the huge mass of Asia. In fact, it covers less than half the area of the United States. But...

■ more than one billion people live there. That's about one fifth of all the people in the world.

■ There are three big nations, as well as several smaller nations. One of the big nations is Pakistan (pack-ih-STAN), with more than 95 million people. Another is Bangladesh (bahn-gluh-DESH), with more than 100 million. By far the biggest nation is India, home to more than 750 million people.

■ India is the world's biggest democracy in number of people. It is a nuclear power—one of the few nations that has exploded a nuclear device. Most of India's people are poor, but they are struggling hard to reduce their poverty. What happens in India—and its neighbors—will affect the future of the whole world.

The people of this important area are not all alike. Many different groups live here. Some have been here since the dawn of history. Others moved in over the centuries. Some came in peacefully. Others came marching in with swords in their hands.

The people speak hundreds of different languages. What's more, followers of nearly all of the world's major religions can be found on the Indian subcontinent. Some families live easy lives with everything they could want. Many others live on city sidewalks with nothing but the rags they wear and a few pots.

Still, the story of these many different people is really one story. They share a piece of land that has done a lot to shape the way they live.

Most parts of this area have one thing in common. The seasons change in almost exactly the same way year after year. That's because of winds known as *monsoons*, which start blowing in from the ocean in late spring. These winds bring rain for about three months. After that, the land slowly dries out. By the spring, it is crumbling into dust.

The monsoon rains make farming possible over much of the subcontinent. And farmers everywhere follow much the same schedule. Every year they wait impatiently for the rains so they can start growing their food again. Eight out of 10 people in the subcontinent make a living from farming. Most people there follow the same basic pattern of life.

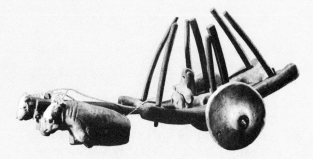

A priest-like figure carved in stone, a clay ox cart with driver, a stone seal with unicorn and writing—all from the Indus Valley civilization. Page 16: Hindu god Shiva, in the dance of creation and destruction.

No one knows for certain how Indian civilization started. But it has been going strong for well over 4,000 years. It has survived wars, invasions, floods, and famines—the worst that people and nature could do to it. Of all the world's surviving groups, only the Chinese can claim a civilization as old as India's.

Indian civilization has left its mark not just on Asia but on the whole world. In many parts of Southeast Asia, you can see ancient buildings in the Indian style. Religions which started in India are now practiced all over Southeast Asia. Some Southeast Asian languages were influenced by India. Even the music of Southeast Asia shows Indian influences.

The Indians never conquered other nations by force. Instead they spread their ideas peacefully. These ideas included two of the world's major religions. One was Hinduism (HIN-doo-iz-um). At one time, Hinduism was the religion of most Southeast Asians. The other religion was Buddhism (BOO-diz-um). Buddhism has died out almost completely in India. But it is still important in other parts of Southeast Asia and in China and Japan.

In the West too, India has left its mark. Long ago, Europeans found this wonderful place far to the east. They knew it first as a place of luxury goods—sugar, spices, fine fabrics. Much later, the British moved into India and governed it for over two centuries. In the end, Indians struggled and won their independence.

Indian civilization is still leaving its mark on the West today. Many Americans keep themselves fit with *yoga* (YOH-guh)—exercises borrowed from the Hindu religion. Many Indian words have crept into the English language. These words range from a burglar's *loot* to your *dungarees.*

MAP EXERCISE

The Indus Valley civilization lasted from about 2500 to 1500 B.C. Use the map to answer the following questions:

1. Find the Indian subcontinent on the world map, page 214. In what part of the world is it located?

2. The Indus Valley civilization began over 4,000 years ago. In what part of the Indian subcontinent was this civilization located?

THE INDIAN SUBCONTINENT

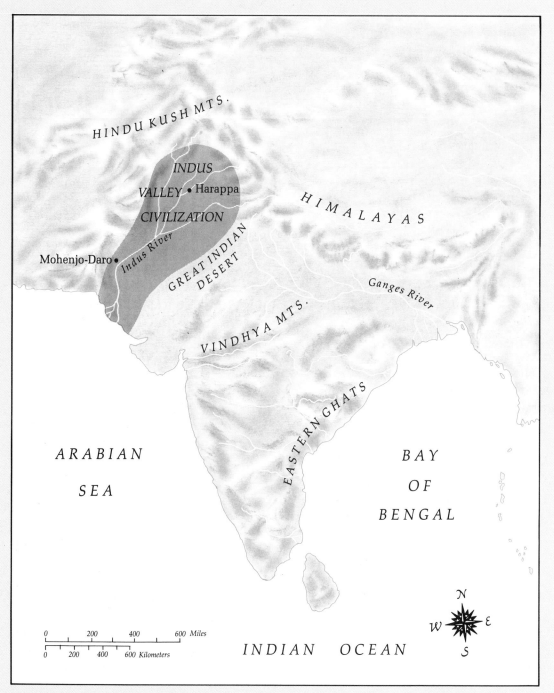

1
Indus River Civilization

The time: the present.

The place: site of Mohenjo-Daro (mo-HEN-joh-DAH-roh), the ancient Indian city on the Indus River in Pakistan (see map page 21).

The scene: three American students—Ava, Eddie, and Sam—are touring the ruins with an Indian guide, Chitra Ghadkari (CHIT-rah GUD-kuh-ree).

MS. GHADKARI: Good morning and welcome. Before we begin our tour, let me tell you why your teachers wanted you to visit this spot. Mohenjo-Daro was one of the world's first cities. It and Harappa (hah-RAHP-uh), another city about 400 miles northeast of here, were part of one of the world's first great civilizations. *Archaeologists* (ahr-kee-AHL-uh-juhsts) found the cities in the 1920's, both of them by accident. Archaeologists are scientists who study the remains of things left by peo-

ple who lived long ago. Harappa had many of its bricks taken away by railroad workers and local villagers. They had no idea that they were destroying the remains of an ancient city. Mohenjo-Daro, however, had never been disturbed.

EDDIE: Who lived here?

MS. GHADKARI: The Indus Valley people. We call them Harappans after the first city to be uncovered. We're not sure where they came from originally. Some scientists think that they may have come from Iran or Mesopotamia. Then, for hundreds of years, they lived in villages and farmed the land of the hilly country near the Indus River Valley. During that time they learned to bake mud bricks for making buildings. Then they moved closer to the river and built walls to protect themselves from floods. Once they lived near the river, they used its rich soil for farming and its waters for irrigation. They also fished in the river and used it for trade boats.

AVA: When was this?

MS. GHADKARI: Experts think the Indus River Valley civilization lasted from about 2500 to 1500 B.C. During the first 300 years or so the people became good builders and *artisans*, or crafts-workers. They also developed their farming and trading. The civilization probably was strongest about 2100 B.C. The whole settlement extended about 1,000 miles north and south along the Indus River Valley. Now, shall we look around one of the world's first cities?

STUDENTS: Sure. *(They start walking.)*

MS. GHADKARI: You probably would not get lost here, even without me. Do you know why?

SAM: Because you always could see those big buildings high up in the center of the city?

MS. GHADKARI: That would help. Both here and in Harappa, there is a central mound or platform made of brick or dirt. We call it a *citadel* (SIT-ah-dell). Many of the cities' most impressive buildings were on citadels. But even without the citadel, you could find your way around. That is because Mohenjo-Daro is laid out in a grid. It has intersecting streets much like New York, Chicago, or Los Angeles.

SAM: How many people lived here?

MS. GHADKARI: About 40,000. But we have to guess based on such things as the number of houses. Let's look at one of the houses before we head to the citadel.

EDDIE: How do you know these were houses?

Mohenjo-Daro was one of the two main Indus Valley cities. Present-day diggings have uncovered a well-ordered town, with impressive homes and public buildings.

MS. GHADKARI: Come see. *(They enter the remains of one house.)* From the street, it *would* be hard to tell there was a house here. Why? Because there were no windows on the side facing the street.

AVA: Why not?

MS. GHADKARI: Maybe for privacy. Maybe to keep the sun out. Maybe even to discourage thieves. But inside there was plenty of light and air. That area was the courtyard and you can see a window facing onto it.

SAM: Still, these could have been stores or some other kind of building.

MS. GHADKARI: There are other clues. Come see the bathrooms.

SAM: Bathrooms?

MS. GHADKARI: The people who lived in Mohenjo-Daro were way ahead of their time in keeping clean. See, this house has an area with waterproofed bricks. There is a sit-down toilet there. And over there is a bathing area with a drain. The people probably bathed standing up, pouring pitchers of water over themselves. The drain is connected to a system of clay pipes. The clay pipes lead to brick-lined sewers along the street.

AVA: Let's go see the citadel now. *(They pass down several streets and reach the central area.)*

MS. GHADKARI: This two-story brick building is known as the Great Bath. Experts think the big bathing pool was for the common people and the little rooms were for a favored class. They think that washing here was part of a religious ritual. Look how everything is built. The bricks are so perfectly placed that you still can't slip a thick piece of paper between them.

SAM: Is anything known about Harappan religion?

MS. GHADKARI: Some of the clay objects archaeologists have found show figures that might give us clues. Two figures seem very important. One is a mother-goddess of the earth and the other is a three-faced, horned god. But we don't really know much about Harappan religion. The main reason is that we don't understand their written language. Some archaeologists have been trying to understand it for many years. Fortunately, they have many examples to work with. Some of the best are on these small carved pieces called *seals*. *(She holds out a small one-inch square of soapstone she has brought with her.)*

AVA: How beautiful. Is that an elephant?

MS. GHADKARI: Yes. Others have water buffalo, apes, tigers, crocodiles, parrots, and rhinoceroses on them. Above each picture is a line of writing in picture symbols.

EDDIE: What were the seals for?

MS. GHADKARI: People probably used them to mark things they owned. The seals themselves also may have been used as part of a system of payment. We know that the people used a system of weights and measures. That, along with the fact that the seals have turned up elsewhere, shows that the people of Mohenjo-Daro traded with people

Soapstone seal of goddess wearing sacred horns receiving a mythical beast—part human, part bull, and part ram.

of other cities.

AVA: What did they trade?

MS. GHADKARI: The farmers grew barley, wheat, peas, melons, and dates. Experts think the Indus people were the first to grow cotton and to spin it and weave it into cloth. They raised chickens, pigs, cattle, sheep, and goats for their meat, milk, and wool. They also made some statues of stone and bronze, some pottery, tools, jewelry, and furniture inlaid with precious metals. Any or all of these things might be traded to other peoples.

AVA: We know the language is a mystery. Are there other mysteries?

MS. GHADKARI: There is the biggest mystery: What happened to the Harappans? Was there some kind of flood or drought? Did the population grow too large to be supported? It seems that the civilization grew weaker slowly. The final blow may have come from invaders from the northwest who had better weapons. Whatever happened, the Harappans were gone by 1200 B.C.

SAM: So these ruins are really all that's left of a people who lived so well for 600 years?

MS. GHADKARI: Yes, although some experts believe that they moved on to other areas. In that case, they would have carried bits of their culture with them to other parts of India. This would mean, in a way, that there are Harappan roots to many of our Indian ways. Just which of our ways may have 4,500-year-old roots will give you something to think about as you continue your study of India's history. Shall we go back to our starting point and look at some of the small objects archaeologists have uncovered? I'm sure you're ready to get out of this hot sun.

✎ Quick Check

1. *Who built the city of Mohenjo-Daro? When? Where is it located? Why were these people considered ahead of their time in keeping clean?*

2. *Give two reasons why it would be hard to get lost in Mohenjo-Daro?*

3. *What do we know about Harappan religion? Why don't we know more?*

4. *What are seals? What were they used for? Describe some of the things the Indus Valley people traded and made. What were they the first to do?*

2
One Religion—and Many

The Hindu religion may be as old as the Indus Valley people described in the previous chapter. The cow is sacred to Hindus—and cows appear in many Indus Valley works of art.

Hinduism does go back to a people known as the Aryans (AR-ee-enz) who began moving into India around 1500 B.C. They came from the northwest. They believed in many *deities*, or gods and goddesses. Each one controlled a different part of nature—the sun, fire, thunder, and so on.

Beginning around 1000 B.C., these people wrote many hymns and prayers to their deities. The writings are known as Vedas (VAY-duz). (The word *veda* means "knowledge.") The Vedas are like the Hebrew and Christian Bible. Hindus today still look on the Vedas as an important part of their religion.

Hinduism is one of the oldest religions in the world. It has changed a lot over the ages. It means many different things to different Hindus. And you cannot really follow the story of the Hindu people without understanding their religion.

A European traveler is talking with a Hindu scholar. "Tell me what Hinduism is," the traveler asks. "And please make your explanation short and simple."

The Hindu smiles. Westerners want everything to be made simple for them. "I will not *tell* you. I will *show* you Hinduism," he says.

They are walking through a village. The Hindu points to a hut. A man is sitting outside eating. "Did you see the man put some rice to one side?" asks the Hindu. The traveler nods. "He will not eat that rice. It is a gift to a deity. You will

The dagger-flashing Indra, among the oldest of Indus Valley deities, fought, gambled, and wore fancy clothes.

also notice that his meal is just rice and vegetables. Like most Hindus, he never eats meat, fish, chicken, or eggs."

"Why is that?"

"Hindus believe that all life is sacred. Look over there." The Hindu points at a cow, which is walking freely down a street. "There are many people in this village who don't always get enough food. But they would sooner starve than eat beef. The cow is the symbol of our protection of all creatures big and small."

27

A woman walks out of a hut carrying bundles. "There is one of my cousins," says the Hindu. "Where are you going, Rukmani?" he asks.

"To the Sacred River," she replies.

"Where is that?" asks the traveler. "Why is she going?"

"She is going on a *pilgrimage*, or journey, to the holy city of Benares (be-NAR-eez)," says the Hindu. "There she will bathe in the holy river, the Ganges (GAN-jeez). By doing that, she hopes to wash away her sins."

"I see," says the traveler. "So a Hindu tries to avoid sin. They follow rituals. And they worship deities. By the way, are there many deities?"

"Oh yes." The Hindu points to an old man who is squatting by the road. The man wears only a cloth around his waist and sits as still as a rock. "That man worships a powerful god called Shiva (SHE-vah). The followers of Shiva avoid pleasure. They eat and drink very little. Some, like this old man, make themselves sit in painful positions."

"So all Hindus avoid pleasure?"

"Oh no. The followers of some other deities believe that pleasure is a necessary part of life."

The traveler frowns. "And how many deities are there?"

"Well," says the Hindu, "there may be 30, or 300, or three million. We can't tell, because one deity may take many forms. Hindus can choose whatever

One of the three main gods of Hinduism, all-seeing Shiva, creates music with two of his many hands while another wields the knife of destruction.

deities they want to worship. No one has tried to count them."

"Then how can you say that Hindus have *one* religion?"

The Hindu smiles. "Because there is one great deity above the rest, Brahman (BRAH-muhn). Brahman has no contact with this world. We cannot know Brahman directly. We do not even know that Brahman is a deity. Some people call Brahman the Absolute. The other deities are a link between this world and the Absolute. And Hindus can choose the links they prefer."

The traveler is silent, trying to understand. Then the Hindu points to another man squatting on the ground.

"Ah," says the traveler, "another follower of Shiva?"

"No," says the Hindu. "He is a *yogi*. He is doing exercises called yoga. He is not trying to make his body uncomfortable. Instead, he is trying to control it. Some yogis can even control the beating of their hearts."

"Is yoga just exercise?"

"No, it is more. It is a way of putting religion into practice. A yogi believes that controlling his body helps free his mind. In the end, he hopes his mind will be free enough to reach the Absolute."

"So all serious Hindus are yogis?"

"Not at all. There are many different paths to the Absolute. Some Hindus worship their deities. Some set out to do good actions. Others study in order to think clearly."

"I see. All Hindus want to reach the Absolute, but they can take different routes." The Hindu nods. "Then is reaching the Absolute like going to heaven when you die?"

"Not quite. For one thing, we believe that we are born on this earth many times. If we do good in our lives, we get closer to the Absolute each time. If we lead evil lives, we will be born again on a lower level. We will have to live and suffer much more."

"I see," says the traveler. "So people such as the yogi and the follower of Shiva are trying to move ahead quickly?"

"Right. They hope to get close enough in this life so they won't be born again on a lower level."

"What did you mean when you said 'born again on a lower level'?" asks the traveler.

"Well, it depends how bad you were in your previous life. You might be reborn as an animal. More likely, you would be reborn into a lower caste."

"And what is a caste?"

The Hindu smiles. "That is a whole new story," he says.

✎ Quick Check

1. *Who were the Aryans? When did they begin moving into India? Describe their religion, and define Vedas.*

2. *What is the cow a symbol of for Hindus?*

3. *How many deities are there in Hinduism? What is the name given to the one great deity above the rest?*

4. *What are some different paths to the Absolute? According to Hindu beliefs, what happens to us after we die?*

3
The Caste System

From almost the beginning of civilization in India, people were divided into four groups or *castes* (kasts). At the top were the priests and scholars. Below them were the rulers and warriors. Next came the merchants and farmers. Finally, there were the peasants and servants. Some people didn't belong to any of these groups. These were the untouchables, the lowest of all.

Over the ages, the castes split into more and more groups. No one is quite sure how and why. Probably, new groups were formed by people who had the same kind of job. Today there are about 3,000 different groups.

Today in India it is against the law to discriminate against someone because of caste. Some untouchables have become government leaders, college professors, and airline pilots. But the caste system is still strong, especially in the villages.

Why has this system lasted so long? One reason is found in the Hindu religion. Hindus believe that they should accept the level of life in which they are born. They should not fight against it. If they lead good lives, then they will be born into a higher caste in the next life (see Chapter 2).

The following story describes how the caste system worked in practice. The story is partly based on fact.

The time: about 1500 years ago.
The place: a village in northern India.

Santha (SON-tuh) hurries along the dusty village street. She is supposed to be at home. Her brother Rama (RAH-muh) is studying the *Bhagavad Gita* (bahg-uh-vad GHEE-tuh), a religious book, with his tutor. Santha is supposed to be sitting in on the lesson. But she knows the tutor doesn't really like teach-

ing girls, and besides, she doesn't like having to sit and listen.

She stops outside the perfume store. As she is looking at the jars of scented oils, she hears a wooden rattle. The street sweepers are coming to clean up the dung left by the oxen. The sweepers are untouchables. They wave a wooden rattle wherever they go. That warns other people the untouchables are coming.

People in the upper castes are not even supposed to see an untouchable.

Santha turns away from the untouchables with a smile. Once she stayed and peeked at the sweepers. It's true, they wore rags and looked very dirty. But did her mother really have to get so upset? Just because Santha looked at the sweepers, she had to wash her eyes out with perfumed water. And her mother

31

wouldn't let her out of the house again for days.

When the sweepers have gone by, Santha runs to the village gate. Beyond the woods, she can see the rice fields by the river.

An ox cart is rumbling toward the village. It's driven by Din, the oil merchant's son. He is a handsome, lively boy. Santha steps back, half hiding be-

hind a tree. Din laughs and waves at her. Santha steps away from the tree and waves back at him. She watches the cart as it rolls into the village.

There is a rustling behind her, but she doesn't hear it. Unknown to her, Rama is there, keeping an eye on her. Santha strolls home.

"Come here!" Her mother sounds angry. Rama walks past Santha, giving her a sly grin.

"What is it, Mother?"

"Santha, did you wave at a merchant boy?"

Santha begins to feel uneasy. Now she understands why her mother is angry. "Yes, Mother," Santha says. "He greeted me as he drove past, and I waved back. He's very handsome."

Santha's mother throws up her hands in despair. "Santha, will you never learn? That boy belongs to a lower caste. You must have nothing to do with him."

"Why?"

"Because we all stay with our own castes, that's why! When you marry, it will be with a boy from our priest caste."

Santha puts on an innocent look. "But Mother, I've heard of a few people marrying outside their castes."

Her mother scowls. "There is some rotten fruit in every basket! Those people usually come to a bad end. Their own people will have nothing more to do with them."

"What does that mean?"

"Look, Santha. If we are in trouble, we can go to anyone else in the priest caste for help. We can do that anywhere. In another village, or in a city. It's the same with the other castes. A merchant can get help from other merchants anywhere. But if you're an outcaste, no one will help you."

Santha thinks for a brief moment. "Wouldn't it be easier if everyone helped everyone else?"

Her mother shakes her finger angrily.

"Santha, we belong to the highest caste. We have gone through many lives to get here. Other people must do the same."

Santha puts on an innocent look again. "Is that why it's all right for a priest to kill a servant?"

"Santha! It is *not* all right! Where on earth did you get that idea?"

"Well, I heard of a priest who got angry and hit a servant. The servant died. And the priest only had to pay a small fine. I think it was the same amount as for killing someone's dog."

"Well, that's different. Priests are not supposed to kill anyone. But of course it would only be a small fine for killing a servant."

"And if a servant killed someone in the priest caste...?"

Her mother raised her hands again. "Don't talk of such things! A servant who strikes a priest must be punished. That's enough talk from you, my girl. You keep quiet and help me make dinner. Or you won't go out again today *or* tomorrow."

Santha is angry, but she says nothing. She thinks that *she* would like to strike someone in the priest caste—Rama, her brother.

✎ Quick Check

1. *What is a caste? How many different castes are there today?*

2. *Why has the caste system lasted so long?*

3. *What is the* Bhagavad Gita?

4. *Who are the untouchables? How did they warn others that they were coming? Why?*

33

4
Siddhārtha Gautama and Buddhism

The time: the present.

The place: the home of Tara Mehrotra (meh-ROW-tra), aunt to Rita and Shama.

The scene: Rita and Shama have come to visit their aunt, bringing a friend, Pankaj (Pan-KUDG).

RITA: Aunt, we have brought a guest.

SHAMA: This is our friend from school, Pankaj Mutsuddy. He has heard what a good storyteller you are and he wishes to meet you.

PANKAJ: I'm very glad to meet you, Tara Mehrotra.

TARA: And I you, Pankaj Mutsuddy. Welcome to my home.

SHAMA: You promised to tell us about Buddha today, Aunt.

TARA: Did I? Ah. Well then, I mustn't dis-

appoint you. Does Buddha interest Pankaj as well?

PANKAJ: Very much.

TARA: Then I will tell you a little about him. You know, there are many stories about the Enlightened One—that's what Buddha means. His followers told these stories, called *jatakas* (jah-TAHK-as), as part of Buddhist teachings. I know some of these stories, but today let us start with who Buddha was and what he taught. The beginning is rather like a fairy tale. Long, long ago—about the year 563 B.C.—a boy named Siddhārtha Gautama was born near the town of Kapilavastu (kap-ih-lah-VASS-too) in the foothills of the Himalayas. That area is called Nepal (nay-PAHL) today. His father

Buddhism began in India and spread throughout the Far East. This ancient Buddhist painting comes from the walls of an Indian cave.

was a warrior prince and his family was rich and powerful. As a child Siddhārtha Gautama must have had whatever he wanted. When he was 20, his parents arranged for him to marry a princess named Yasodhara (you-SO-drah). It seems that Siddhārtha Gautama was not happy with his ordinary, comfortable adult life. He was troubled by the suffering and unhappiness he saw around him. Suddenly, when he was 29, he left his wife and his very young son, Rahul (RAH-hool).

RITA: But why? What for?

TARA: As I have said, he was not satisfied. It is said that he had four visions or dreams. In the first one he saw an old man; in the second he saw a sick man; in the third he saw a dead man; in the fourth he saw a wandering holy man. It was that last vision that made him leave his family. He shaved his head, put on simple clothes, and set out to discover the secret of release from suffering.

PANKAJ (eagerly): And he found the secret, didn't he?

TARA: Not just then. Such secrets are not easily discovered. He wandered for six years. During that time he talked to great religious leaders. He prayed, fasted, and tortured himself. One day when Siddhārtha was 35, he sat under a large bo (boh) tree, where he said he would stay until he learned how people could become free from life's suffering.

PANKAJ: And then he discovered what he was looking for?

TARA (nodding): Some say he sat there for a few hours. Some say that he sat there for many days. Then at long last he understood the secret of unhappiness. He preached his first sermon under that tree. Then he spent the rest of his life spreading his message to the common people. His message was important to the history of our country and to the history of many other countries of the world. It came at a time when people were looking for new religious ideas, for something that was not so harsh and hard to understand as Hinduism.

RITA: But his message, Aunt. What was it?

TARA: He believed that the cause of suffering was the desire for worldly goods, for wealth and power. But he believed that people could behave so that they could free themselves of worldly attachments. Then they could achieve great peace and happiness. He called this freedom from suffering nirvana. After this, Siddhārtha Gautama was called Buddha.

SHAMA: And what does one do to reach nirvana?

TARA: One follows what Buddha called the Middle Way. That is a life in which one neither gives in to all worldly longings nor has to torture oneself. There is an in-between way of life that encourages people to be kind to others and all living things. Buddha said, "May none deceive another, or think

As a young boy Siddhārtha Gautama lived like other children. Here he rides in a chariot, perhaps to school.

ill of him in any way whatever, or in anger or ill-will desire evil for another."

SHAMA: Surely that is not all—be kind to one another?

TARA: No, although that is an important message, don't you think? Buddha had a plan for self-control. He called it the Noble Eightfold Path. These are the eight steps of the path: one, knowledge of the truth; two, the intention to resist evil; three, saying nothing to hurt others; four, respecting life, morality, and property; five, holding a job that does not injure others; six, striving to free one's mind of evil; seven, controlling one's feelings and thoughts; and eight, practicing proper forms of concentration.

PANKAJ: But how does one put each of those things into practice?

TARA *(laughing):* For the answer to that,

37

Pankaj, you must go to a *guru* (GOO-roo), or religious teacher. I am only a storyteller. But, of course, you understand most of the steps. And you can see that there could be different ways to understand some of them. Step five has to do with an important part of Buddha's teaching—something called *ahimsa* (uh-HIM-sah). Ahimsa is the belief that it is wrong to harm any other living creature, human or animal. This teaching meant that no Buddhist could be a hunter or a butcher. Buddha said, "May every living being, weak or strong, large or small, seen or unseen, near or far, born or yet unborn—may every living thing be full of joy."

SHAMA: But the story, Aunt. What happened to Buddha?

TARA: As I said, he spent the rest of his life spreading his message. He had many followers who also spread his message. These *monks* dressed in orange-yellow robes and gave up their homes, as Buddha had done. They traveled, begging for food and teaching Buddha's message. Buddha himself preached his message until he became ill and died at the age of 80.

PANKAJ: But Buddhism went on?

TARA: Oh, yes, for more than 1,000 years. Buddha had planted the seeds of something very powerful. He preached a message that was more simple and more hopeful than that of Hinduism. One simply followed the Eightfold Path to find happiness. Buddhism drew many, many followers. Yet, in the end, it died out in India.

RITA: Why is that, Aunt?

TARA (*shrugging*): The Hindu priests were stronger. But they borrowed many of Buddha's beliefs and made them part of Hinduism. Ahimsa, for example, became part of Hinduism.

SHAMA: But there are still Buddhists?

RITA: Yes, we learned in school, remember? There are many Buddhists in China, Tibet, Japan, and other countries.

TARA: Yes. Although Buddhism did not last here, it spread throughout Asia. And, although it has changed since it began in India, Buddhism is one of the world's great religions.

PANKAJ: You said you know some other stories about Buddha. Will you tell them to us?

TARA: Not today, young man, although I will tell you another if you come again. I enjoy telling stories about our country and its past to young people. Now I must get on with my work. Come again soon, all of you.

✎ Quick Check

1. *Why did Siddhārtha Gautama leave his comfortable life? What did he finally realize was the cause of all suffering?*

2. *What is nirvana? How does one reach it?*

3. *What was Buddha's plan for self-control called? Name at least three steps of the path.*

4. *How did the teachers of Buddhism spread his message? What happened to Buddhism in India?*

5
The Mauryan Empire

The time: the present.

The place: the living room in Myna's house.

The scene: Myna and her classmate, Dilip, are studying together at a table.

MYNA: I'm glad we're studying together, Dilip. Let's get started.

DILIP: Okay. Tomorrow's test covers the Mauryan (MOW-re-uhn) Empire—or as our teacher calls it, one of our more glorious periods.

MYNA *(nodding):* The Mauryan Empire dates from 321 to 185 B.C. It was the first Indian empire to provide central government for almost the whole country. Its center was the Ganges (GAN-dgeez) River, on the opposite side of India from where our civilization began. See what I mean? *(She points to a map like the one on page 51.)*

DILIP: Right. Now here's how India was unified: About the time of Buddha there were at least 16 kingdoms in northern India. They often fought with each other. In 322 B.C. Chandra-gupta (CHUHN-druh-GUP-tuh) Maur-ya came to power. We don't really know much about his background. He was Aryan, like many of the leaders in those times. He used his army to take over the rest of northern and central India—everything but the southern tip. The lands he took made up the Mauryan Empire.

MYNA: It was larger and stronger than any Indian kingdom had been before. It lasted about 150 years. And that's saying something, because transportation and communication weren't very fast or well organized then. It must have been hard to hold all that land and all those people together under one ruler.

DILIP: So what comes next?

MYNA: During its early period the Mauryan Empire was governed very strictly. Its citizens had few freedoms. The government used spies to check on citizens' loyalty. Crimes were punished severely.

DILIP: On the other hand, the way of life improved greatly for many of the people. They worked on farms, in the forests, and in mines. In workshops, artisans made cloth, jewelry, and things from wood. Public *irrigation*, or channeling water for farm use, helped farmers grow larger and better crops. Merchants traded Mauryan-made goods and farm products with Ceylon, Greece, Rome, Malaya, Mesopotamia, and Persia.

MYNA: The capital was Pataliputra (pah-tuh-lih-POO-truh), which is now Patna. It was surrounded by walls with 570 watchtowers and 64 gates.

DILIP: Now let's get to the interesting part of the test. Two thirds of it will be an essay question: "Who do you think was the greatest Mauryan leader and why?" I'll do Asoka (ah-SO-kuh). Which one would you like?

MYNA: You know there is only one other leader of great importance. All right, I'll do Chandragupta, which means I go first. Let's see. First I'll review the facts. Chandragupta Maurya ruled from about 321 to 298 B.C. He took over much of northern India, and what is now western Pakistan, and part of Afghanistan. I think he was the greatest

Mauryan ruler for two reasons. One, he accomplished the hardest task, taking over all that land and putting together one large empire. Two, he was tough, which was necessary. Ruling with an iron hand was what held the kingdom together and brought it wealth and peace. All in all, he was the perfect leader for his time.

DILIP: That's one way to look at it. Some people say he was cruel and unjust. Better tell about his spies again and about his book on how to rule.

MYNA: I was coming to that. He had an army of 70,000 soldiers with 9,000 elephants and 10,000 chariots. The army protected merchants who traded with other countries. The trade helped the cities grow. A well-to-do class of merchants and traders owed their comfort to that army.

DILIP: And where did the money to pay for this army come from?

MYNA: Chandragupta made sure that there was plenty of money for governing his country. A certain share of all the grain produced in the land went to the government. What's wrong with that?

DILIP: Nothing, unless you happen to be a farmer. The farmers on those lands were not allowed many pleasures, such as celebrating religious festivals. It also wasn't so great if you were a poor family and your land was taken by the government. But then Chandra-

Buddhist relics are kept in a dome-roofed stupa (far right). Carved figures in the gate leading to the stupa tell the stories of the Buddha's previous lives.

gupta didn't care much for the common person, did he?

MYNA: Individuals may have suffered a little, but their taxes gave them army protection.

DILIP: And if you didn't pay your taxes?

MYNA: You were severely punished. What was he supposed to do—ask people to please pay a little money?

DILIP *(sighing):* Don't forget to mention the book and Kautilya (KOW-till-yah).

MYNA: All right, all right. The book was *Arthashastra* (ARTH-ah-sha-strah), a famous book on how to govern. Experts think Kautilya, an advisor to Chandragupta, wrote it. It tells exactly how to rule. For example, it tells how to take over groups on the edge of the empire. First, spies mingled with the people. They got to know the leaders of the groups. Then they spread rumors or did whatever else was necessary to turn the leaders against each other. While the group was weak, Chandragupta's army moved in and added the land to the empire.

DILIP: A nice way to treat one's neighbors!

MYNA: Oh, and let's not forget that Chandragupta also used tax money to build and improve roads and canals, which helped everybody. Your turn, now, Dilip. What will you say about Asoka, who was, after all, Chandragupta's grandson?

DILIP: I will make it clear that he was an improvement over his grandfather, for one thing.

MYNA: Of course, he didn't have to put together his own empire. He inherited one from his father and grandfather.

DILIP: Myna, give me a chance. First, Asoka Maurya ruled from about 273 to 232 B.C., when he died. We know a lot about him because he had his deeds and ideas carved into rocks and stone pillars. I think he was the greatest Mauryan leader for three reasons. He had the courage to change his ways when he thought it was right to do so. He was a man of peace. And he sent *missionaries* to other countries to spread the Buddhist message. Many faiths have such people who carry their beliefs to new lands.

MYNA: He had no interest in making the Mauryan Empire larger? He had no army? His soldiers never killed in the name of the empire?

DILIP: In the early days of his rule Asoka was not so different from his grandfather. He ruled according to the *Arthashastra.* He sent his soldiers to fight against neighboring kingdoms. He expanded the empire far into southern India. Then he changed. No one knows exactly why, although Buddhist priests had something to do with it. In one Mauryan war against a neighboring kingdom, about 100,000 people were killed. Many others starved to death or became ill as a result of the effects of the war. After that, Asoka said he would fight no more. He became a Buddhist and changed his government to reflect Buddhist beliefs.

Brahma, one of 3 main Hindu gods. His heads grew to let him watch his beloved with whom he created the human race.

MYNA: You'd better give some examples.

DILIP: He tried to be at peace with neighboring groups. He encouraged people to treat each other and animals kindly. He accepted people of all backgrounds and beliefs. He apologized to the peoples he had fought. He set up hospitals. He forbid animal sacrifices and protected wildlife. He had his workers plant shade and fruit trees, dig wells, and make resting places along trade routes. He changed the laws so that they would be more fair to the common citizen. In other words, he tried to rule on the basis of his religious beliefs. And he also sent Buddhist missionaries to Ceylon, Burma, Central Asia, and China, which was very important to the spread of Buddhism.

MYNA: But he kept his army, just in case he needed it?

DILIP: That is true. And it is also true that the Mauryan Empire lasted only 50 years after his death. Still, while he was alive, he did much for his people. I certainly would rather be remembered for the things Asoka did than for the things Chandragupta did.

MYNA: Mmmm. In any case, we both need some kind of conclusion for our essays. I think I will say that the Mauryan kings, of whom Chandragupta is an excellent example, were political experts. They united all Indians.

DILIP: And I will say that the Mauryan kings, of whom Asoka is an excellent example, spread one culture, the Aryan culture, as they spread their empire. And that was important for uniting all Indians.

MYNA: And good luck to both of us on the test!

✎ Quick Check

1. *Who united most of India into the Mauryan Empire? How long did the empire last?*

2. *What were some of the benefits of living in the empire? What were the drawbacks?*

3. *Who was Asoka Maurya? How was he different from Chandragupta?*

4. *What was the Arthashastra?*

6
The Golden Age of the Guptas

In 320 A.D., an Indian leader who called himself Chandra Gupta I, after the Mauryan Chandragupta (see Chapter 5), rose to power. He was the first in a line of rulers from the Gupta (GOOP-tuh) family. Their empire lasted about 180 years, until 500 A.D. It came to include all of northern India and parts of central and southern India. Its capital was at Pataliputra on the Ganges River, which also had been the Mauryan capital.

The Guptas brought a *golden age* to India. A golden age is a time when there is great growth in art, literature, education, religion, and science. Usually such growth takes place when there is a strong government, or a time of peace, or a group of well-to-do citizens. For most of the time during Gupta rule, India enjoyed all three of these conditions.

Active Religious Life. The Gupta rulers were Hindus, but the people followed the teachings of both Hinduism and Buddhism. For the Hindus, two gods, Vishnu and Shiva, were very important. Vishnu was thought of as a kind god who worked to make the world better for all who lived in it. Shiva's task was to keep order in the world. The Hindus worshiped their deities in many different ways, both in temples and at home.

Under Gupta rule, many temples and monuments to deities were built. Some of the temples came to be thought of as especially holy. They were supported by both the poor and wealthy who worshiped in them. Their money paid for sculpture to decorate the buildings and for the many priests, musicians, and dancers who took part in religious cele-

The love between the beautiful milkmaid Radha and the god Vishnu (here as Krishna) was seen as the perfect union of the soul with god.

brations. Some of the large temples also set up schools and hospitals.

In the temples and in their homes, Hindus worshiped *idols*—statues of deities made of stone, metal, wood, or clay. Since the Hindus believed that the deity was present in an idol, they took special care of it. They clothed it, offered it food, and bathed it.

Indian religion and social customs were closely tied. The caste system (see Chapter 3) continued during the Gupta Empire. By then there were thousands of sub-castes or *jati*. Each person was born into a certain jati, such as the farmer jati or the weaver jati, and was a lifetime member, even if he or she did not actually farm or weave. He or she was expected to behave according to the rules of that jati. That meant marrying someone of the same jati and observing the jati's rules about eating and drinking. The jati were not equal. Some were considered higher or more pure than others.

At the very bottom of the caste system were the untouchables. The caste system divided the Indian people from one another. But it had a purpose. It helped the people divide the work and organize their daily lives.

The Arts Flourish. There was, however, much joy and beauty in Gupta life. Musicians and dancers developed the forms that are the basis for classical dance and music in India today. Sculptors and painters worked on art for temples or monuments. Usually their work showed religious subjects and scenes

from daily life. Great works were written in the Sanskrit language. One of the greatest writers was Kālidāsa (kah-lee-DAH-sah), a playwright and poet. Here are some lines from his famous play, *Shakuntala* (shah-KUN-tah-lah). The plot has to do with a king who has lost his memory. In this scene Shakuntala, the king's pregnant wife, tries to help him recall who she is by describing how they met.

> SHAKUNTALA: Do you not remember in the masjine-bower,
>   One day, how you had poured the rainwater
>   That a lotus had collected in its cup
>   Into the hollow of your hand?
> KING: I am listening. Tell on,
> SHAKUNTALA: Just then, my adopted child,
>   The little fawn, ran up with long, soft eyes . . .
>   And you, before you quenched your own thirst, gave
>   To the little creature, saying, 'Drink, you first, gentle fawn.'

Gupta theater-goers expected to feel a wide range of emotions, but wanted a play to end happily. A play might include as many as eight emotions, known as *rasas*. One scene might make the audience laugh, another might make them cry, a third might make them angry. The other five rasas were pride, love, fear, loathing, and wonder. In the last scene the playwright tried to make the audience feel all eight rasas mixed together in one wave of love-laughter-anger-sadness-pride-fear-hatred-wonder.

The *Bhagavad Gita* was an important book in Gupta times. It actually was part of a larger body of stories called the *Mahabharata* (mah-hah-BAHR-tah). The *Mahabharata* was written hundreds of years earlier, but the Gupta rulers had it rewritten to include Hindu ideas. The *Gita* is a tale about warriors. In it, a warrior named Arjuna doubts his right to kill in battle. The god Krishna tells him that it is his duty to fight and kill, and perhaps to die, since he was born a warrior. The deities will judge him on how well he performs his warrior duties.

Education and Science. Since Gupta India was a center of learning, visitors from other parts of Asia often traveled there. It is from the writings of some of these visitors that we learn more about Gupta life. The Guptas themselves were not very interested in recording history.

One Chinese visitor wrote about a hospital where patients received free care and commented on how humane he thought the Gupta government was. Another Chinese visitor was impressed by the quality of Indian education. In Hindu schools and Buddhist monasteries, students took classes in grammar, mathematics, medicine, philosophy, and religious writings. Young people of many religions came from China and elsewhere to study at the university of the Buddhist monastery at Nalanda.

The field in which Gupta scholars made great contributions to world learning was science. These were a few of their inventions and discoveries:

- **Inoculation.** Indian doctors were the first to give patients shots to prevent diseases such as smallpox.
- **Surgery.** Indian surgeons sterilized their tools. They knew how to set bones. They used plastic surgery techniques to repair ears and noses.
- **Arabic numbers.** Gupta mathematicians invented the decimal (ten-based) number system and the numerals 1 to 9 that we use today.
- **Zero to infinity.** Gupta thinkers developed the idea of zero and wrote it as a numeral. They also had a symbol for *infinity* or endlessness.
- **Textiles.** Gupta workers discovered how to twist cotton fibers into a fine thread. Cashmere, calico, and chintz came from India.

Under the Guptas, some new ideas were introduced and some of the old ways preserved. The Gupta's created a way of life that lasted, with few changes, until modern times.

✎ Quick check

1. *When and under what rulers was India's Golden Age? What conditions allowed it to occur?*

2. *Why are the deities Vishnu and Shiva important to Hindus?*

3. *What are the eight rasas? How did playwrights use rasas to entertain theater-goers?*

4. *Name at least three inventions or discoveries of Gupta scholars.*

7
Akbar the Great

Gupta India did not last. New invaders began moving into India around 1000. These were *Muslims* (MUZ-limz) from central Asia. They were followers of a religion called Islam (ihs-LAHM). They believed it was their duty to spread their religion everywhere.

The Indians outnumbered the invaders, but the Indian armies were poorly trained. They relied too much on elephants—which often ran wild and killed people on their own side. By about 1350, the Muslims ruled most of India.

Most of the Muslim kings ruled harshly. But one was different. This was Akbar (ACK-bar), whose name means "great." He became king in 1556, when he was 13. He ruled much of India for nearly 50 years. Like other Muslim kings, he waged many wars. But he also ruled justly, treating Hindus as equals.

Let's imagine a Hindu clerk in Akbar's palace kept a diary for the year 1581:

FEBRUARY 3. Another bad night. The king ordered me to come to him at 4 A.M. He sleeps only three hours a night in the best of times. And these are *not* the best of times.

He dictated a letter to one of his army commanders. Where are his soldiers? They should have arrived at the capital city days ago. The rest of the army is already here.

Sometimes I wonder if the king's life is safe. I'm sure some of his Muslim generals are plotting against him. They don't like the way he makes friends with the Hindus. Muslim leaders before him taxed us heavily. But Akbar is very fair with his Hindu subjects. He even lets us worship in our own way. I think it's partly because he married Hindu princesses.

Lately, Akbar seems interested in *all* religions. Last year, he wrote to the Portuguese colony on the coast. He asked

Akbar defeated many states to unite India. Here his troops storm a fortress.

48

them to send some Roman Catholic priests. He wanted to talk with them about Christianity.

Two priests have been here ever since. The king often talks with them. I don't think he's becoming a Christian. I know he's not a Hindu. But I'm sure he's no longer a Muslim. That's why there's this rebellion in the northwest. The king's own half brother is leading it.

If the king doesn't crush the rebels, some of his own generals might join them. Because of this, the king is taking no chances. He went over to talk with some of the generals this afternoon. Then I had to go with him to the cannon factory. He's very interested in the making of guns. He wanted to check that they were being made properly.

In the evening the king asked me to read to him. Strange that he can't read himself—he's a very gifted man. Some people say that as a boy, he spent too much time learning to fight and hunt to learn to read. I read some Indian history to him. But he listened for only about 10 minutes. He's very restless.

We're all restless. It's like sitting on one of those cannons. Akbar has talked of marching north to put down the rebellion of his half brother. The whole kingdom could explode at any moment.

AUGUST 26. News at last. A messenger arrived this morning from the northwest. King Akbar won the battle. His army drove the rebels back. Now it is chasing them out of India.

The king will not try to kill his half brother. "He is my flesh and blood," says the king. "He has not treated me like a brother. But I must treat him like one."

I was very proud that the king sent a special message for me. He asked me to keep an eye on his palace artists. He wants me to criticize their work once a week as he always does. I don't think the king needs to worry. He has some of the best artists this country has ever seen. There are over a hundred of them now. Some of them paint wonderful portraits. Some paint animals and birds. Others are expert at illustrating books. Some of the art of the palace is against Muslim beliefs. The king tries to combine the best of both the Muslim and Hindu worlds.

DECEMBER 1. A familiar voice boomed through the palace. The king is back.

He called for me this afternoon. He has all kinds of plans for the future. He wants to change some of our old Hindu ways. For example, he plans to end child marriages by law. Now young girls won't have to marry much older men. Very traditional Hindus won't like that. But they will be delighted with another law he will pass. He is going to ban the killing of cows for food. That is something we Hindus have always wanted done.

I wish he would take care to please his Muslim subjects as much. But it seems the king has turned against his own Muslim religion. He is going to ban the building of new *mosques* (mosks), the Muslim houses of worship.

Conflict between Akbar and other

Muslims did not end with time. In 1605, he was murdered by his own son. The son, Jahangir, was angry at his father because he had abandoned his Muslim faith. Jahangir poisoned Akbar and took the throne. He inherited one of the most powerful empires in the world at that time.

✎ **Quick Check**
1. *When did the Gupta Empire end? Why?*
2. *Who was Akbar? What did he do that was different from other Muslim rulers of India?*
3. *When did Akbar become king? How long did he rule?*
4. *How did Akbar die? Why?*

INDIA EXPANDS

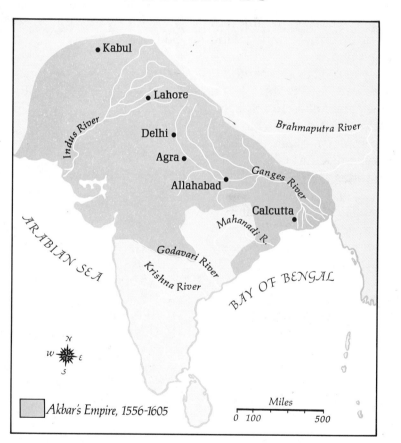

Akbar's Empire, 1556-1605

Akbar ruled much of India for nearly 50 years. Use the map to answer the following questions:

1. What two major river systems were part of Akbar's empire?

2. Describe the location and boundaries of Akbar's empire.

PART 1
Review and Skills Exercises

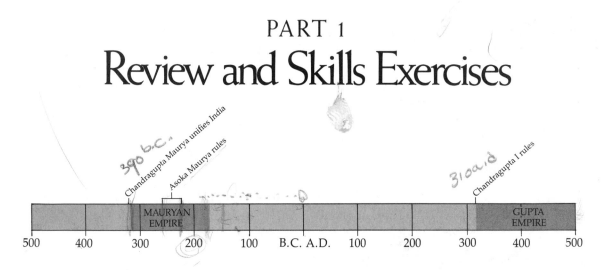

Time line showing: Chandragupta Maurya unifies India; Asoka Maurya rules; MAURYAN EMPIRE; Chandragupta I rules; GUPTA EMPIRE. Handwritten annotations: 390 b.c.; 310 a.d. Scale: 500, 400, 300, 200, 100, B.C. A.D., 100, 200, 300, 400, 500.

Using a Time Line

Part 1 described events in India from the twenty-fifth century B.C. to the seventeenth century A.D. This long span of history includes the rise and fall of great empires. During this time, India was changed by religions, invaders, and powerful rulers. The time line above shows events between the years 500 B.C. and 500 A.D. Use the time line to answer the following questions.

1. In what century did Chandragupta Maurya unify most of India?

2. In what century did Asoka introduce Buddhist ideas into the government?

3. About how many years did the Mauryan Empire continue after Asoka's death?

4. The Guptas brought a golden age to India. About how many years did it last?

5. About how many years after Chan-dragupta Maurya ruled, did Chandra Gupta I come to power?

Understanding a Tradition

When invaders take over a territory, they usually bring many changes with them. This was true of the Muslims who came to India in the eleventh century A.D. They brought the Islamic religion. They also brought traditions, or ways of doing things.

A Muslim tradition that took hold among many Hindus was *purdah*. Purdah is the practice of keeping women secluded, or hidden from view. Women were kept behind high walls. They were not to be seen by men outside their families. Often, women wore veils in the presence of their husband's brothers.

Here is how a woman in purdah acts and dresses: She spends most of her time inside the walls of her home. She is careful to stay covered in her garden where others might see her. When she leaves home, she covers herself with long clothes. Muslim women wear a long covering called a *burka*. The burka covers a woman from head to toe and has eye-slits to see through. A Hindu woman covers her face with the end of her *sari*. A sari is a long cloth that is worn wrapped around the body. It is the traditional garment of Hindu women.

A woman in purdah rarely goes to public functions. If she does, she might sit behind a screen so as not to be seen.

Not all Muslims practiced purdah and it was mostly the upper-caste Hindus who took it up. The practice of purdah has declined, but there are still places where one can see women in long dark robes with their faces covered.

Imagine what it was like for an Indian woman who had grown up in purdah to be told she could be seen in public without a veil. It was not an easy change for some. Here are the words of the wife of a Hindu town official who gave up purdah in 1919:

> I was invited to attend a party held by some officials of the government. I can't go, I protested. I knew there would be many men around and I would feel terribly shy. My husband persuaded me to go. I found that I enjoyed myself, but I was still too ill at ease to shake hands with other guests or to drink my tea.

Answer the questions that follow.

1. What is purdah and how did it come to India?

2. How do you think the practice of purdah restricted the lives of women?

3. Why was it difficult for some women to give up purdah?

Building Vocabulary

Write the numbers 1-6 on a sheet of paper to correspond to the six sentences below. By each number write the words from the list that best complete each sentence. There is one extra word you will not need.

Muslims
Harappa
India
Pakistan
Vedas
Shiva

Mohenjo-Daro
Buddha
Akbar
Hindu
Bangladesh
Siddhārtha Gautama

1. The Indus River Valley was the home of two ancient cities named _____ and _____ .

2. Today the Indian subcontinent contains the three large nations of _____ , _____ and _____ .

3. The _____ are important writings of the _____ religion.

4. In the sixth century B.C. _____ _____ left a comfortable life to seek an answer to how humans can find release from suffering, and became known as _____ .

5. Around 1000 A.D., people from central Asia who were _____ moved into India and established an empire.

6. _____ the Great ruled India from 1556 to 1605 and is remembered for his wise and successful rule.

PART
2

ANCIENT CHINA

Two powerful rivers start in the mountains of inner Asia and flow across the continent. In the fertile mud that these rivers laid down during countless floods, farming began as early as 3000 B.C. On these flood plains grew a great civilization—the Chinese.

The northernmost of these two rivers flows through dusty plains. The powdery soil there is yellow. It gives a yellow tint to the waters of the network of small rivers that sweep it away. These rivers join to form the Huang He (hwang huh), meaning "Yellow River." The Huang He dumps its yellow mud into the Yellow Sea.

Further south, the second major river is called the Chang Jiang (chahng jahng), or Long River. The powerful waters of the Chang Jiang have cut deep gorges through Asian mountains. As they near the sea the waters become calm. They flow across fertile plains where grain stalks nod lazily in the warm sun.

Chinese civilization in the northern river valley began at least as early as Indian civilization—perhaps earlier. We know that 3,700 years ago a Chinese kingdom flourished in the north. Smaller Chinese groups settled near the Chang Jiang, to the south. Other non-Chinese groups lived nearby.

As in other parts of the ancient world, rivers attracted settlers. They provided highways for travel. They furnished water for drinking and for growing crops. China's rivers flooded regularly—two years in every three. Each flood left a layer of mud on nearby fields. The mud built up a rich soil in which crops grew well.

The floods also brought danger to human life. They spurred families and clans to organize into larger groups. These groups built dams to control the floods. They also built systems to irrigate their crops.

No one knows exactly when the first Chinese communities formed. Chinese stories and legends tell of kings and wars that, if true, must date back beyond 2000 B.C. Remains have been found to prove some of this. Writing was invented around 1700 B.C. What happened earlier is more difficult to know for certain.

The Chinese thought of themselves as a sort of giant family. At the head of the family was the king (or later, the emperor). Such rulers are *monarchs* (MAHN-arks). They inherit their power. A family that rules for many generations is known as a *dynasty* (DIE-nuh-stee). A single dynasty might include several rulers. Each ruler was usually the son of the one be-

56

Clay figures, like the kneeling woman and warrior from 200 B. C., were buried with the dead in place of live people. Model of a miller's shop contains first example of a hand crank in left wall. Page 54: Zhou dynasty bronze vessel.

fore. The Chinese had 10 major dynasties before a revolution drove out the last emperor in 1911.

Early Accomplishments. The Chinese were fiercely proud of the civilization they developed. They had many reasons for this pride. Among them were:
- Writing
- Painting (began to develop about the time of Jesus)
- Paper (first developed about the same time)
- Gunpowder (invented soon after)
- Printing (became common in China between the seventh and tenth centuries A.D.)

Such achievements show the richness of Chinese civilization. They help to explain why China became the "mother culture" for all of East Asia. Other peoples, such as the Japanese, the Koreans, and the Vietnamese, based their own cultures on Chinese ways.

The ancient Chinese believed that their civilization outshone all others. They called their nation Chung Kuo (joong gwoh), meaning the middle or central kingdom. Other kingdoms were thought to revolve around theirs. People outside Chung Kuo lacked the benefits of Chinese civilization. To the Chinese, such people were "barbarians."

MAP EXERCISE

Dynasties ruled China for almost 4,000 years. Use the maps to answer the following questions:

1. Find the region that is Chinese on the world map, page 214. Describe the area's location.

2. What trend do the four maps show?

3. Which dynasty was the first to include the Chang Jiang River region?

4. Which dynasty was centered around the Huang He River area?

5. Was the area ruled by the Han dynasty larger or smaller than China today?

6. Most of the work on the Great Wall was completed between 220 and 210 B.C. Which dynasty ruled China at that time?

CHINA GROWS

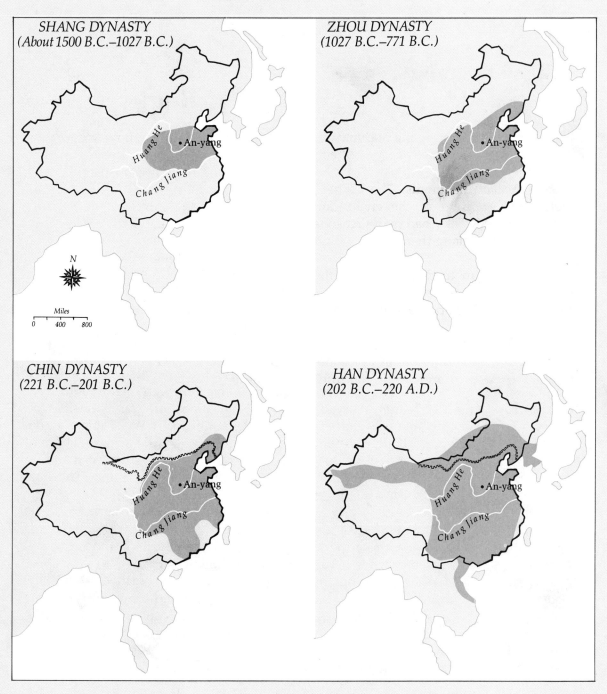

SHANG DYNASTY
(About 1500 B.C.–1027 B.C.)

Huang He
• An-yang
Chang Jiang

N

Miles
0   400   800

ZHOU DYNASTY
(1027 B.C.–771 B.C.)

Huang He
• An-yang
Chang Jiang

CHIN DYNASTY
(221 B.C.–201 B.C.)

Huang He
• An-yang
Chang Jiang

HAN DYNASTY
(202 B.C.–220 A.D.)

Huang He
• An-yang
Chang Jiang

8

The Dragon Bones of An-yang

To learn about China's early history, some scholars have turned to "dragon bones." The bones did not really come from dragons, of course. Dragons are make-believe animals. Rather, "dragon bones" are the name modern Chinese gave to a special type of bone that they found. They ground these bones into a powder for curing sickness.

About 100 years ago, scientists studied the bones. They found that they were marked with ancient writing. Excited, the scientists believed that these markings provided clues to China's past. Worried that such evidence was being destroyed, the scientists tried to stop the use of "dragon bones" as medicine.

Many "dragon bones" were actually the collarbones of cattle and other animals. The ancient Chinese used "dragon bones" to try to peer into the future. They took bones to certain people called *soothsayers*. Such people were believed to have magical powers. The soothsayers wrote questions on the bones. "Does trouble lie ahead?" "Will I make a good marriage?" "Will the rains come soon?" Then, the soothsayers placed a red-hot rod into a hole in the bone. The bone cracked. By studying the cracks, the soothsayers worked out answers to the questions.

During the 1920's, thousands of "dragon bones" turned up in a dig at An-yang (ahn-yahng), north of the Yellow River. An-yang had been China's capital from 1300 to 1135 B.C. Along with other evidence, the "dragon bones" showed what life must have been like in China at that time.

60

The Shang Dynasty. The findings at An-yang and elsewhere tell of a dynasty of kings called the Shang (shahng). This is the first Chinese dynasty for which considerable proof exists. It began about 1500 B.C. and lasted until about 1027 B.C. The Shang was one of the many royal families in China. Different dynasties ruled smaller Chinese kingdoms to the west and south. The Shang kingdom was one of the largest and most powerful.

During the Shang dynasty, artisans made fine bronze work and delicate carvings in marble and jade. They used the wheel for war chariots and in making

Workers sort silkworm cocoons from which they will later draw thread.

pottery. Also, they developed an advanced system of writing.

Farmers then grew crops similar to those they grow now. In the dry north, farmers grew a grain called millet. In the wetter and warmer south, they grew rice. Many families also grew mulberry trees. Silkworms fed on the leaves and spun cocoons. By unwinding the silkworm cocoons, the Chinese got delicate fibers which they wove into cloth. Only nobles were allowed to buy and wear silk cloth.

Chinese silks are among the softest and finest fabrics ever made. Centuries later, Chinese merchants began to trade silk to Europe and the Middle East. But they kept the secret of making it to themselves. Rome and the city of Alexandria in Egypt fought over precious silk cargoes. Laws were passed to govern who could wear it. Famous women like Egypt's Queen Cleopatra adorned themselves with it.

Chinese society divided people into three separate classes. The first class was the *aristocracy* (air-uh-STAHK-ruh-see). It included kings and nobles. Great warriors also belonged to the first class. Artisans and merchants belonged to a second class.

The third class was made up of farmers. Then, as now, most of China's people worked the land. Most of them did not own their land, but rented it from a noble family. Most had only small plots, crowded together. They had only crude wooden tools to use. If they were lucky,

*Jade carving of a child and an old man
watching a farmer till his field*

they managed to grow enough food to pay the rent and feed their families. In times of drought and flood, they often starved.

Even in the time of the Shang, the Chinese had closely-knit families. Children were taught to respect and obey their parents and grandparents. This was called *filial piety* (FIH-lee-uhl PY-uh-tee). They were also taught to admire and respect their ancestors—back through many generations.

Filial piety and respect for ancestors were linked. Parents knew that someday they would die. They wanted to make certain that their children would honor their spirits. So they raised their children to respect their elders unquestioningly. The older the parents became, the more honor they received. For this reason, most Chinese looked forward to old age.

62

In addition to the ancestral spirits, the Chinese believed in many other spirits. They thought different kinds of spirits were everywhere and could bring luck or harm. They did not worship these spirits as deities. Rather, they saw them as annoying or helpful neighbors who needed attention and respect.

The Chinese also worshiped many different deities. The most important one was Tien, the god of Heaven.

During the Shang dynasty, there were many complicated religious ceremonies. One of the most important ones took place whenever a king died. Before he was buried, his servants and guards were sometimes killed. It was believed that they would serve and guard him in

*A terra cotta infantryman, one of an
army found in the tomb of an early emperor*

the afterworld. After the Shang rule of China ended, this practice slowly died out.

The Shang kings ruled for over five centuries. But, eventually, the dynasty grew weak. Meanwhile, a pioneering people from the west were gathering strength. Finally, these rugged farmer-soldiers, the Zhou (joh), overthrew the Shang and established a new dynasty.

Power from Heaven. To justify grabbing power, the Zhou royalty claimed that they had been chosen by Heaven to rule. This right to rule was called the Mandate (command) of Heaven. Supporters of the Zhou dynasty said that the Shang kings had not taken care of the people. Angered, Heaven had withdrawn its mandate from the Shangs and given it to the Zhous. Zhou kings called themselves the "Sons of Heaven." From then on, whenever a dynasty fell, the new rulers would say that Heaven had taken its mandate away from the old rulers.

When the Zhou rulers took over, they were strong and ambitious. They began to expand Chinese territory. For the first time, the Middle Kingdom stretched southward to include parts of the Chang Jiang valley. It expanded to the west and north as well.

The Zhou rulers could not govern all their land by themselves. Instead, they set up smaller local governments, run by nobles who were usually friends and relatives. These local rulers gave the chief ruler their loyalty and soldiers during a war. In return, the local rulers were allowed to collect taxes.

In 771 B.C. the Zhou capital was overrun by *nomads* (NOH-madz), or wanderers, from the west. The government moved its center south, but it lost the loyalty of its nobles. China became a land of four great states and about 60 small ones. Over the years the states developed strict codes of honor for dealing with one another. These applied especially in warfare. Soldiers competed with one another to see who could be the most honorable.

As the smaller states became absorbed by the bigger ones, the courtesy of warfare began to break down. By 335 B.C. the big states were locked in a struggle to the death. Surprise attacks and the killing of prisoners replaced old rules of fair play.

In this time before China became united again, Chinese thinkers puzzled over the problems of their society. How could people live in peace and harmony with one another? What was the proper way to run a family and a nation?

✎ Quick Check

1. *What are "dragon bones," and how did the ancient Chinese use them? What have scientists learned from "dragon bones?"*

2. *What was the earliest dynasty about which we have a lot of information? Describe its social order and religious practices.*

3. *How long did this early dynasty last? How did it end?*

4. *What was the Mandate of Heaven? Which dynasty "invented" it? How and when did this dynasty lose power?*

9
Confucius:
China's Great Teacher

Around 551 B.C., a man was born who would leave his mark on China down to our own time. His name was Kung Fu-tsu (koong foo-tzuh). Kung was his family name. Fu-tsu was a special title, meaning "Grand Master." In the Western world he is called Confucius (kuhn-FYOO-shuhs).

Confucius was born into a family of minor nobles. Stories about him say that he was a respectful son. Like other young men of his class, he studied for a government job. He memorized historical facts and ancient poems. He learned the complex rules of proper behavior.

In time, Confucius became a teacher. But he taught his pupils more than facts and poems and good manners. He tried to teach them a set of rules for proper living. Through his pupils, he hoped to influence government officials to improve their ways of governing.

During his own lifetime, Confucius drew little attention. Few people recognized his accomplishments. But in later centuries, Confucian thought (called Confucianism) would deeply affect Chinese life. Confucianism would become the official *doctrine*, or policy, of China.

Confucius lived in a time when order among the many states was preserved by codes of honor (see Chapter 8). He preached purity, sincerity, self-respect, and respect for others. But only by following proper rituals could one succeed in reaching these goals. Ordinary people should obey and respect their superiors. Children should honor their father, mother, and ancestors.

Rubbing of a stone carving of Confucius from the eighth century

Confucius addressed many of his remarks to rulers. He said:

If the ruler is good and wants only what is good, then the people will be good. The ruler is like the wind. The people are the grass. The grass must bend in the direction the wind blows.

Confucius argued that the government should be run by the most qualified people. Such people did not have to be of noble birth. But they did have to be people of high moral character. And they had to be well-educated.

At the time Confucius lived, the Chinese states were developing a large, highly educated *bureaucracy*, or people who run the government. That bureaucracy continued to grow. In later years, the bureaucracy would set rules that touched almost every aspect of daily life.

Unity under the Chin. In 221 B.C., one of the large warring states finally completed its conquest of all the others (see Chapter 8). This was the Chin. The Chin leader, Shih-huang-ti (Sher-hwahng-dee) was the first to call himself emperor. He was also the first to rule over a truly unified China. He completed construction of a barrier against invasion from the north begun by Zhou rulers. This barrier is called the Great Wall. Wide enough to hold six rows of soldiers on top, it stretched 1,500 miles or more. Parts of the wall are still standing today.

Under the Chin an elaborate code of laws was written. The emperor issued *standards*, or guidelines, to make writing the same all over China. He even made standards for carriages so that roads could be the same width. But the emperor's harsh rule made him unpopular. In 213 B.C. the emperor ordered all Confucian writing burned. He wanted to control the bodies and minds of his subjects.

Only another strong leader could have continued the work started by Shih-huang-ti. His son proved not to be such a leader. After three years, the son had shown his inability to rule. Thus, 20 years after it began, the Chin dynasty came to an end.

The Han Dynasty. In 202 B.C., the Han dynasty came to power. Han rulers differed greatly from Chin rulers. For example, the Chin rulers had rejected Confucian ideas. But during the 400 years of the Han dynasty, Confucianism became the official policy of the government.

Soon an official university was set up. There, students from the landowning class and the aristocracy learned the teachings of Confucius. They also studied a set of even more ancient writings known as the classics. After 132 A.D., all students who wanted government jobs had to pass a standard written exam. This helped to make sure that Chinese officials were familiar with the ideas of Confucius and other Chinese *sages,* or people of great wisdom.

By this time, China's class of nobles had shrunk. The nobility was limited mainly to the emperor's large family. Two new classes had grown up. One was the bureaucracy. The other was a class of well-to-do merchants and landowners.

Only the upper classes knew how to write in Han times. Below is the kind of letter that might have been written then. Most of the values set forth in the letter come from the teachings of Confucius.

From Wang Lien, to his son Wang Ping at the university:

Dear Eldest Son:

The entire family is proud of your success. You are the first of the Wang family to pass the second stage of the government examinations. Now you can look forward to an honorable life of service to the emperor.

Our family does not come from the nobility. But we are respectable people. We are used to working with our minds, not with our hands. Therefore, we are among the natural leaders of society.

Today your grandmother heard of your success. Right away she walked to the family tomb in the hills near our house. She said a prayer of thanks at the graves of your grandfather and our other ancestors.

You will find as you grow older that your respect for your family and ancestors will repay you. For only people who know how to behave with those close to them will know how to act with strangers.

You must rule yourself. Then you can rule others. You must be kindhearted toward those who are under you. And you must be loyal to those above you. Treat others with the respect you give yourself. Do not do to others what you would not want them to do to you.

Above all, you must not go to extremes. A hot temper shows that a person is not in control of himself. If you can't control yourself, how can you govern others?

Your younger sister shows perfect behavior. Last week she was walking with your grand-

Officials prove their worth by writing Confucian essays before the emperor.

"The Family Visit" shows the ideal relationships within the family as taught by Confucius: children helping their elders, women behind the men.

mother. By chance they passed the man she will marry next spring. Yet she walked on without any sign that she knew the man. For a 15-year-old, she is very sensible.

I believe my choice of a husband for her was a good one. Though I made my decision 12 years ago, I still do not regret it. Naturally your sister has said nothing. But I believe she too is pleased with her intended. Next spring we will welcome you home for the wedding. As an important official, you will add honor to the family ceremony.

I know you will make a worthy servant of your emperor. In the old days, our rulers too often governed by force alone. That kind of rule is right only for barbarians. It is not right for the most powerful and civilized nation un-der Heaven. Princes now rule by good example. This way they prove they have the Mandate of Heaven.

> Your affectionate father,
> Wang Lien

✎ Quick Check

1. Describe the times in which Confucius lived.

2. What were Confucius's main teachings? According to Confucianism, why was self-control important?

3. What was the first dynasty to unify China? When? What were its accomplishments? How long did it last?

4. When did Confucius's teachings finally gain official support in China?

10
China's Many Paths to Truth

Picture a spring day in ancient China. Small family groups are making their way through a cemetery. Each family stops before the grave of an honored ancestor. Respectfully, the people kneel at the grave. From baskets they remove cakes, fruits, and other foods. They place the foods on the grave to pay *homage,* or respect, to the ancestor.

The practice of paying homage to ancestors is sometimes called *ancestor worship.* It is an ancient Chinese tradition. Its roots extend back long before the time of Confucius. The early Chinese believed that the spirits of dead ancestors survived in a spirit world. If treated with respect and honor, the ancestors' spirits might talk to the deities. They might influence the deities to grant health and wealth to members of the family who remained on earth.

Ancestor worship has continued to be part of China's life. It has mixed with other beliefs and traditions. We will look at four types of Chinese belief from Han and pre-Han times. Some of these beliefs, like ancestor worship, have to do with religion. Other beliefs are concerned with what is right and wrong. These beliefs—which include Confucianism—are more correctly called *philosophies* (fuh-LAHS-uh-feez).

Law above All. After Confucius died in 479 B.C., followers worked to spread his ideas. But many important people did not like Confucianism. A group of thinkers called the Legalists offered a rival set of laws.

The Legalists did not share the Confucians' faith in education. Confucians believed that people could be taught to be good. Legalists believed that people must be forced to be good. They placed their faith in strict laws, which were strictly enforced.

What's more, the Legalists did not share the Confucians' deep respect for social differences. Confucians believed that some people were naturally superior because of their virtue or birth. Superior people included rulers in the nation and parents in the family. Rulers and parents were due complete respect and obedience. They were not subject to the same rules as other people. For example, they could avoid punishment for certain wrongdoings, while a peasant could not. For Legalists, however, the law was the law. It must apply to everyone.

In 221 B.C., when the Chin took power, the Legalists got a chance to put their ideas into practice. Top officials of the Chin dynasty were Legalists. They developed a harsh system of laws. It was Legalist thinking that was behind the emperor's order to burn the classics, including the writings of Confucius. Such ancient books, claimed the Legalists, were dangerous. The classics confused people and weakened respect for the law.

Confucians, as we have seen, had deep respect for the great writers of the past. They hated the Legalists. And Confucians soon had their revenge. Under the Han dynasty, which followed the Chin, Confucians gained power. Legalists lost their influence.

Over the centuries, many new ideas became part of Confucianism. Some Chinese came to worship Confucius as a sort of god. But this was not part of Confucius's teachings. Confucius was mainly a philosopher and not a religious thinker.

In the centuries that followed the life of Confucius, two major religions gained followers. One, called Taoism (DOW-iz-im), began in China. The other, Buddhism, came from India.

Harmony with Nature. Taoism comes from the word Tao (dow). Tao means the Way, or the Path, to happiness. Believers in Taoism seek to bring their lives into harmony with nature. They seek to understand nature's way, or rules. By following those rules, they try to find inner peace.

Unlike Confucianism, Taoism pays little attention to government or formal education. Instead, it encourages people to *meditate*—to think quietly about the universe and about simple events in nature. Here are the words of the founder of Taoism, Lao Tzu (lau tzuh):

Without crossing his threshold
He knows the whole world;
Without looking from his window
He perceives the ways [tao] of Heaven.

Taoism teaches people not to reach for fame or fortune, but to be content with what they have. At the same time, Taoists criticized the government for letting some people have too much food while others starved.

Taoism won many followers among people who were fed up with the constant wars of the third and fourth centu-

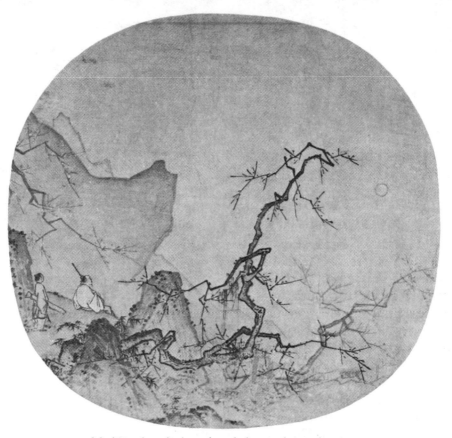

Ma Yüan's painting of a scholar studying the moon
through the bare branches of a plum tree

ries B.C. It appealed to people who wanted peace and quiet. But it also expressed a hopelessness about people in society. Observing the disorder around him, one Taoist philosopher wrote: "What is the life of man, where is the pleasure? Dead, he is stinking corruption, but how much worse eternal life!"

A Hopeful Religion. Another religion reached China in the first century A.D. This religion was Buddhism (see Chapter 4). Buddhism was introduced in China by merchants. About this time a brisk trade was developing along the Silk Road between China and the western parts of Asia. Chinese traders carried Chinese silks, cinnamon, and furs. On the return trip they brought cloth and exotic goods not found in China. These goods included dyes for coloring and alfalfa seeds. The traders also brought new ideas about religion.

Those were difficult times in China. The Han dynasty was weakening. Civil war had broken out. During these troubles, many people began to question the teachings of Confucianism and Taoism. Seeking answers to their questions about life, many turned to the new, foreign religion—Buddhism.

71

A Chinese pilgrim to India returned in 645 with packloads of Buddhist writings gathered during 15 years of study there (above). Images of the Buddha (left) are often in this peaceful, seated pose.

Over the centuries, Buddhism almost died out in India. But it took root in China. At first the Buddhist teaching—not to strive for worldly rewards—seemed familiar to the Chinese. It was considered a form of Taoism. But gradually it became a separate religion in its own right. The Chinese were attracted by beautiful Buddhist art. They loved the wonderful stories of the goodness of famous Buddhists. Most important, Buddhism offered a way to salvation. It was a way out of the suffering of daily life.

As the years went by, artists made many statues and paintings of the Buddha. Buddhist monasteries became centers of religious thought. From China, the faith spread to Korea and Japan. Buddhism enriched the cultures of those nations as well.

✎ Quick Check

1. *According to Chinese belief, how does ancestor worship benefit the Chinese family?*

2. *What are the two main differences between the ideas of Legalists and Confucians?*

3. *During what dynasty were the Legalists in control of China? What policies did they favor?*

4. *What do Taoists believe? How do they differ from Confucians?*

5. *When and how did Buddhism reach China?*

73

11
Spreading the Word

The early Chinese gave much thought to the search for truth. They meditated and prayed. But they also took a strong interest in the world about them. They wanted to invent things that made daily life better and easier. In time, they became famous for their skill as inventors.

One major Chinese invention was the art of printing. The Chinese mastered printing six centuries before Europeans did. No one person can be given credit for the original idea. Many details of the development of printing have been lost. But we have a good idea of how it came about.

Making Copies. During the Han dynasty, rulers who honored Confucius wanted to make a permanent record of his thoughts. One emperor ordered 46 slabs of stone set up in his capital. On them, sculptors carved the words of Confucius. People could then come to read the thoughts of the great teacher.

Soon people thought of copying writing that was carved on stones. So they pressed a thin sheet of paper against a stone. Then they rubbed the back of the paper with a chunk of charcoal. Everything except the words came out dark. Scholars could make their own "prints" of the master's words.

But this was slow work. And it could only be done with messages carved in stone. Over the centuries, some Chinese wondered if there wasn't a better way of making copies.

According to tradition, a better way was invented. This is how it was done. A

Even today, writing is a fine art in China. Scholars (right) are copying old works to make new books for the emperor's sons.

scholar would first write on thin paper, with ink and a small brush. While the ink was still wet, the paper would be pressed down on a block of smooth wood. When the paper was peeled away, the writing would be seen backward on the wood. A worker would then take a sharp knife and carve around the words, or *characters*. With pieces of wood whittled away, the characters would stand out.

Then the printer applied ink to the raised characters and pressed down on them with a sheet of paper. The result was a copy—no longer backward—of the original writing. A skilled printer could do as many as 2,000 sheets in a day. This new printing invention meant that many more people had books to read.

As far as we know, the world's earliest printed book was made in China. It is dated 868 A.D. It contains pictures of the Buddha along with religious writings. Each page was printed from a single slab of wood.

Later, printers made books with *movable type*. That meant that smaller pieces of wood, clay, or metal contained one character rather than a page of characters. The printer could arrange many characters to make a page. The printer could rearrange the same characters to print other pages.

Writing with Symbols. A Chinese printer had to have several thousand separate pieces of movable type on hand. The reason was that the Chinese do not have an alphabet such as the one we use.

Rather, each Chinese character stands for a word. There are thousands of different characters.

Some characters are simple. For example, the symbol for *tree* is written this way: 木 . Even a beginning student would have no trouble remembering that character.

Sometimes, characters are simply combinations. If 木 is *tree*, then 林 is *forest*. Or the character for *sun* 日 might be combined with *tree* 木 . The result is: 東 . It means *east*, because the sun is first seen through the trees as it rises in the east.

Some things, of course, can't be shown with a picture. For example, *sincerity*. How would you draw a picture of sincerity? Pretty hard. So Chinese scholars invented this complicated character: 誠 .

The writing system played a huge part in the spread of Chinese culture. For one thing, the written language helped to bring all parts of China together. In fact, the written language unified China more than the spoken language did. Chinese was—and is—spoken differently in different parts of China. But, on paper, Chinese can be read the same way everywhere.

The written language also produced a rich literature. It helped to maintain the values that we now think of as Chinese. Chinese writing was even used outside of China's borders. In time, the writing system spread to lands like Korea, Japan, and Vietnam.

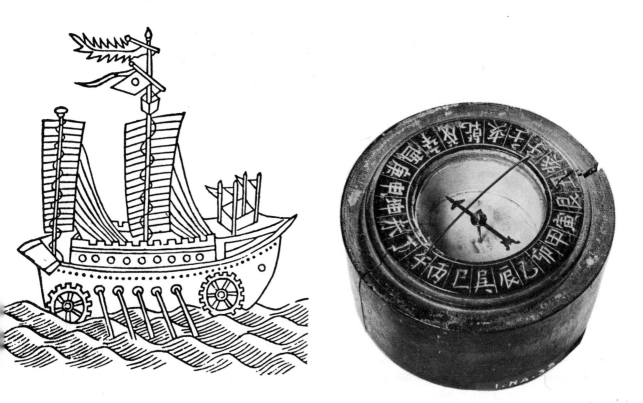

The paddlewheel boat and the compass are among the many inventions credited to the Chinese.

Other Inventions. Along with printing, other Chinese inventions spread to the far corners of the world. The secret of paper-making traveled into western Asia and later into Europe. The magnetic compass, invented in China, reached Europe through Arab travelers. Gunpowder was another Chinese invention. When the outside world learned the secret of gunpowder, the course of history was changed.

✎ Quick Check

1. *Describe the methods used in printing the first Chinese book.*

2. *What later improvements helped the Chinese to speed up the work of printing?*

3. *How do Chinese methods of writing differ from our own?*

4. *How did the writing system help to unify China and spread Chinese culture? What other inventions besides printing came from China?*

PART 2
Review and Skills Exercises

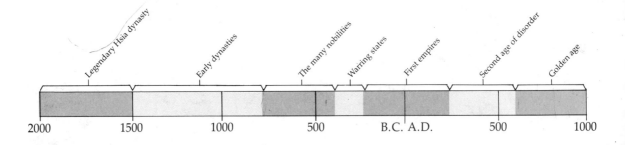

Legendary Hsia dynasty — Early dynasties — The many nobilities — Warring states — First empires — Second age of disorder — Golden age

2000   1500   1000   500   B.C. A.D.   500   1000

Understanding Events

You have read many facts about China in Part 2. Rulers, dynasties, and changes in society and government were described. This information, and some additional facts, have been organized in two different ways in these skills pages. The time line above orders events into periods of time. The chart on the next page shows information in a different way. Study the time line to answer the following questions.

1. If Chinese stories and legends are true, when did the Hsia dynasty rule?

2. When Buddhism reached China in the first century A.D., did it bring the golden age?

3. Confucius was born in 551 B.C. During what period of time did he live?

4. How many centuries did the early dynasties rule?

5. During what age was the first book printed?

6. How many centuries of China's golden age does this time line show?

Using a Chart

This chart lists some of the early developments in China. Study the chart and answer the questions that follow.

1. What types of information about China will you find in the chart?

2. What period of time does the chart cover?

3. During which dynasty did the following develop?

    a. the domestication of animals

    b. ancestor worship

    c. Confucianism

4. How was the wheel first used?

5. If you wanted to know the number of years between the first dynasty and the first empire, would you use the time line or the chart?

Building Vocabulary

Each of the sentences below can be completed by using one or more of the words that follow it. Write the numbers 1-5 on a sheet of paper. Next to each number write the word or words that best completes each sentence.

1. Two rivers that have shaped the history of China are the _____ and the _____ .

Chung Kuo   Shang
Huang He   Chang Jiang

2. Ancient Chinese fortune tellers used _____ to try to peer into the future.

mulberry leaves   "dragon bones"

3. Beliefs in early China included respect for family elders called _____ and the practice of honoring ones ancestors known as _____ .

ancestor worship   filial piety
dynastic cycles   Taoist rules

4. _____ in China were members of a ruling family, or _____ .

bureaucracy   dynasty
monarchs   mandates

5. In the West we know this person by the name Confucius, but in China his name is _____ .

Tien   Anyang
Zhou   Kung Fu-tsu

DYNASTY	CULTURE	ART	RELIGION AND PHILOSOPHY
HSIA 2000–1500 B.C.	millet and wheat cultivated potter's wheel used animals domesticated	black pottery	
SHANG 1500–1027 B.C.	writing invented cultivated silk worms for silk used the wheel on war chariots	white pottery fine bronze worked marble and ivory carved jade and turquoise used	belief in spirit world filial piety ancestor worship
ZHOU 1123–256 B.C.	astronomy advanced crossbow invented	lacquer	Confucianism Taoism
CHIN 221–202 B.C.	Great Wall built		Legalism official policy
HAN 202 B.C.–222 A.D.	iron sword used soybean cultivated	wall painting sculpture	Confucianism official policy

PART
3

CHINA GROWS WHILE JAPAN RISES

Word passed like wildfire among the farm families of central China. "A great canal to be built . . . Report for duty . . . By the emperor's orders . . . To start at once . . . " The people groaned when they heard the order. Why must they bear this new burden?

The farmers were very poor. Most of them owned no land. The land they worked belonged to great landlords. Each year, a large share of the crop went directly to the landlord for rent. Farm families were lucky to feed themselves until the next harvest. Many families went hungry. In bad years, many starved.

And now this. The emperor had ordered that rivers must be widened and channels cut to make a great canal. All men between the ages of 15 and 50 had to work as laborers. Each family also had to provide a child or an old person to help prepare the workers' meals. To open a channel, the workers had to carry the dirt away one basket at a time. It was an enormous task. At least a million people worked on the canal.

Finally the first Grand Canal was completed in 618. (A second one was built around 1300.) It connected the rich southern lands near the Chang Jiang to the yellow northern plains near the Huang He.

The Grand Canal was a great burden to the farmers. But it helped to bring about an age of prosperity. It was built at the start of a new period of unity. After the Han dynasty fell in 220 A.D., China became divided once more. The northern part of the country was taken over by nomadic tribes. The Sui (sway) dynasty in 589, re-united the country. This dynasty built the Grand Canal and helped to knit together the northern and southern parts of China.

Two other dynasties governed China during the next six centuries. The Tang dynasty ruled from 618 to 906. It helped to build up China's trade. It also encouraged the growth of arts and culture. After a period of civil war, the Sung (soong) dynasty ruled from 960 to 1279. It repaired damage done during the civil war. Education became important once again.

Workers pull the boat of a Sung dynasty emperor through the Grand Canal. Page 80: An official succeeds in winning the loyalty of a neighboring state.

Under the Tang and the Sung, China had one of the world's most advanced civilizations. Their technology remained far superior to that of the Europeans. There was a flowering of culture and the arts. Painters, poets, dancers, and singers were respected and well paid. So were the makers of pottery, bronze statues, colored silks and clay figures. The first printed books appeared in the Tang period.

Confucianism and Buddhism enjoyed a period of increased popularity. Despite the differences in these beliefs, their followers lived in harmony. Then in 841 Buddhism came under attack from the Tang emperor. The government seized the property of many Buddhist temples. After that, fewer and fewer Chinese practiced Buddhism.

Contact with Foreigners. Chinese caravans traveled across the deserts of Central Asia. Chinese ports welcomed fleets of ships from the Persian Gulf, India, the Malay Peninsula, and Japan.

This increased contact with the non-Chinese world brought a wave of immigration. Large groups of foreign traders settled in China. There were Muslims from Central Asia, Hindus from India, Zoroastrians from Persia, Christians from Syria, Jews from Arabia, and many others. However, most Chinese wanted to have as little to do with these new people as possible. Big trading cities like Guang-zhou (gwahng-JOH), also called Canton, even set aside special sections for foreigners.

China's superiority was known and accepted throughout the East. Chinese power extended to Korea and part of the present-day Vietnam. Leaders of these peoples paid yearly tribute to Chinese emperors.

The Japanese people never came under Chinese control, partly because their island nation was easy to defend. But all groups were greatly influenced by Chinese culture.

Shifting Population. Within China, certain changes improved the lives of many. Chinese civilization began in the northern plains, near the Huang He. By the end of the Han dynasty, that area was already crowded. Then came invasions, civil wars, and terrible floods that devastated the land. Starving families moved to the south and started life anew. By the time of the Tang dynasty, the south had become China's farming center. There, farmers grew more grain than the local people needed. Boats on the Grand Canal carried the grain northward to those areas with food shortages.

Foreign flags fly above the port of Canton. By the end of the last dynasty, the Ching, central areas of many ports were under foreign control.

The north was still China's center of government. The emperors kept their capitals at northern cities like Chang-an (now Xian) and Loyang. But this area was always prey to nomadic invasions. Once again, in 1126, China lost control over its northern provinces. So the Sung moved its capital to the south.

The nomads who constantly threatened China's northern borders were, in fact, great admirers of the Chinese. But they expressed their admiration by trying to conquer China. While the Chinese could expand their empire, they often could not hold it. For hundreds of years, China would be ruled by non-Chinese.

85

12
Women Lead and Follow

Kao-tsung was a well-meaning ruler, but he couldn't make up his mind. This was his undoing. But his weakness provided an opportunity for another to show her strength. This was the empress Wu.

Empress Wu was named Wu Chao (woo jau) at birth. She was not born into a royal family. At the age of 14, though, she was chosen to live at the court of the great Tang emperor Tai-tsung. A beautiful and lively girl, Wu Chao won the heart of the emperor's son, Kao-tsung.

When Kao-tsung became emperor in 650, he took a proper wife from the ruling class. Wu Chao then tricked the emperor into believing that his wife had committed a terrible crime. Kao-tsung agreed to remove his wife and put Wu Chao in her place.

As the person closest to the emperor, Wu Chao was not satisfied to simply enjoy the luxuries of palace life. She was better at making decisions than the emperor, and so she did.

While Kao-tsung was still alive, Wu persuaded him to lower taxes and to stop spending so much money on the army. Instead, she advised him to spend money on improving farming and the silk industry. These new policies helped make China prosperous.

The emperor died in 683. Seven years later, Wu Chao had herself proclaimed "emperor." She ordered anyone who was in line for the throne to be murdered or sent away.

Despite her cruelty, Wu was an able ruler. Chinese nobles challenged her right to rule even after she took power. So, naturally, she did not appoint nobles as her advisers. Exams were used to find talented, educated people, and she paid them well. All this strengthened the government.

Empress Wu also encouraged artists, writers, and musicians. She was a Buddhist, but permitted others to practice their own religions. She ordered that a

Family life was governed by women, especially the rearing of children who were considered the property of the whole household.

large bronze urn be set out to receive suggestions from the public. Any person who had a complaint could drop a note into one of the urn's four slots.

Eventually, in 705, Wu's right to rule was taken from her. But in 15 years, as China's sole ruler, she had proven that a woman could lead.

The Female Side. Powerful women lived throughout Chinese history. But they usually remained in the background. Part of the reason can be found in the ancient idea of the *yin* and *yang*.

From earliest times, people saw certain rhythms in life. The seasons changed, bringing life and growth in the spring

The yin-yang *circle is divided equally between dark and light. Each of the 8 sets of lines is a word for a family member.*

Bound-footed actresses in performance.

and summer, death in the fall and winter. People saw that opposites such as death and life, dark and light, wet and dry, female and male, were part of nature. They called these opposites the *yin* and *yang*. *Yin* was the female side, *yang* the male. These opposites were thought to balance each other.

Too much of the female side was thought to be more dangerous than too much of the male. These ancient beliefs might have formed the basis of what later became social customs to control women.

By the time of the Tang dynasty, a woman's position was strictly limited. According to one Tang writer, this was how a woman should be:

A chaste [pure] woman must not go out often, but must be ready to obey commands. If asked to come, she must come at once; if asked to go, she must go quickly. If she fails to obey any order, reproach [criticize] her and beat her. . . .

When others are present, she must preserve a modest demeanor [behavior] and, after bringing them tea or soup, walk slowly backward and retire to her own room.

An unfortunate practice for women was the way the family name was continued. A woman did not carry on the family name into which she was born. Rather, she carried on the family name into which she married. To continue the family line was a sacred responsibility of the son. Since a woman could not do this, she was not highly valued by her own family. In her husband's family, however, she might make a place for herself. Women usually outlived men and elders were highly respected. So women could look forward to positions of respect later in their lives.

But because of their lower value as children, too many women never made it to adulthood. In times of hardship, families were known to kill their newborn daughters. Certainly daughters never received as much respect as sons.

Foot-binding. Some time in the Tang dynasty around 950, a new fashion began to take hold. It was to affect the lives of many women for hundreds of years. Some say it was started by a dancer in the royal court. She danced on the tips of her toes on a gold stage shaped like a flower. To make her feet small, she bound them with strips of cloth. This made the toes curl toward her heels.

Over time, other women started binding their feet in this way. Mothers would wrap the feet of their young daughters to assure the smallness of their feet when they grew up. It was painful for the child. It deformed the bones of the feet. But women were willing to make this sacrifice. Why?

Foot-binding had become more than a fashion. It was a sign of wealth and status. Women with bound feet did not and could not work in the fields. In time a woman with bound feet became a romantic prize to a man.

Foot-binding was never common in southern China, but it was widespread in the north. It reached its peak of popularity in the seventeenth century. Unfortunately, women did not follow the example of one of their empresses. She was large-footed and claimed that she needed big feet to pacify the empire. Instead, foot-binding continued until this century.

✎ Quick Check

1. *When did Empress Wu rule? In what ways was she an able ruler? What did she do to seize power?*

2. *Define* yin *and* yang, *and tell how these ideas came about. How might they explain Chinese customs regarding women?*

3. *Why did families consider girls less valuable than boys?*

4. *What was foot-binding? Why was it done? How long was it done?*

13
Japan Borrows from China

In the beginning were the deities. And the deities gave birth to islands—islands that now make up Japan. The sun goddess ruled over the heavens. The storm god ruled over the ocean. Those were but some of the many gods and goddesses. Others ruled over fire, mountains, trees, the moon.

In time, the deities gave birth to human beings. The deities were the ancestors of the Japanese people. Our emperor is a direct descendant of the sun goddess.

That is the way the ancient Japanese described the beginnings of their land and people. That is the story that many Japanese tell even today.

People were living in Japan 10,000 or more years ago. Where they came from, no one can say for sure. They are Asian, like the Chinese. But the Japanese language has little in common with the Chinese language.

Japan lies about 125 miles off the east coast of Asia. In their early history, the Japanese were just close enough to the mainland to be influenced by Chinese culture. Yet they were far enough away to avoid Chinese invasion.

There are as many as 3,000 volcanic islands in the Japanese island group. Most of them are tiny. From ancient times, most Japanese have lived on the four largest islands. Together, these islands equal an area about the size of California. People who live on them enjoy a mild climate.

The Japanese have always been proud of the beauty of their islands. Yet most of them have seen that beauty destroyed more than once. Earthquakes, volcanic eruptions, and tidal waves have plagued Japan for centuries.

Farmers and Warriors. Like China, Japan was mainly a nation of farmers. Mountains and hills left only small areas of flat land. Thus, farm plots were very small. People ate mostly rice and vegetables. Because Japan was surrounded by

One of the beautiful buildings in the city of Heian, now Kyoto, when it was Japan's capital beginning at the end of the eighth century.

seas, the people ate a lot of fish. They raised almost no animals for meat because there was little room for grazing.

For centuries, there was no strong central government in Japan. A Chinese history written about 297 A.D. tells of a queen named Pimiko who could work magic. She ruled over the 30 states of Japan. But she did not have much power. Basically, Japan was a nation of separate *clans*, or groups of related families.

By the sixth century A.D., Japan had an emperor. The emperor was an important religious figure. It was believed that he was related to the sun goddess, and that he could never die. But, like Pimiko, the emperor had only a limited say in politics. The leaders of powerful clans often made the big decisions. In the countryside, each clan controlled its territory.

In 552, a Korean king sent a message to the Japanese. He asked for help in fighting other Korean kings. As a token of good will, the Korean king sent the Japanese some Buddhist writings. He also sent statues of Buddhist saints.

A Great Debate. Buddhism captured the imagination of some clan leaders.

They found in Buddhism the way to truth. They urged the Japanese to adopt the new religion. Other clan leaders were very critical of Buddhism. They said the Japanese must never abandon their traditional religion. This traditional religion involved worshiping deities who represented different forces of nature. Those who practiced it called it Shinto (SHIN-toe), which means "the way of the deities."

Much more than religion was at stake in this debate. Those who favored Buddhism were also attracted by Chinese philosophy and Chinese methods of government. In theory, at least, China had a strong central government. That appealed to Japanese leaders who were tired of the struggles among powerful clans. They wanted to have a central government in Japan. They wanted to reduce the powers of the clans and give the emperor more power.

One man was responsible for helping to settle the religious debate. This was Prince Shotoku, who was an adviser to the Empress Suiko. Shotoku was a Buddhist, and wanted Buddhism to be the official religion. But he stressed that Shintoists should be allowed to practice their religion in peace.

In the end, Shotoku had his way. Buddhism and Shintoism existed side by side. The Japanese even combined some parts of the religions. Buddhists worshiped Shinto deities in Buddhist temples, and Shintoists practiced certain Buddhist rituals.

Prince Shotoku was also responsible for bringing much of China's culture to Japan. In 607, he sent a group of scholars to the great city of Chang-an in China. Over the years, many Japanese went to China to study Chinese learning and customs. They brought what they learned home to Japan.

The Japanese began to wear Chinese-style robes. They patterned their buildings after Chinese buildings. They built a stronger central government. By 900, the Japanese had figured out a way to write Japanese words with Chinese-style characters.

But the Japanese did not swallow Chinese culture whole. They kept many of their old ways, or changed them slightly to fit their own circumstances. For example, the Japanese system of government kept many of its old features. Also, the emperor never had as much power as Chinese rulers. Strong clan leaders usually held power behind the scenes. This system would go on for many centuries.

✎ Quick Check

1. *Describe the traditional religious beliefs of the Japanese.*

2. *Why did some Japanese favor, and others oppose, the introduction of Buddhism and Chinese culture?*

3. *Who was Shotoku? How did he help bring Chinese culture to Japan?*

4. *How did the roles of the Japanese and Chinese emperors differ?*

JAPAN

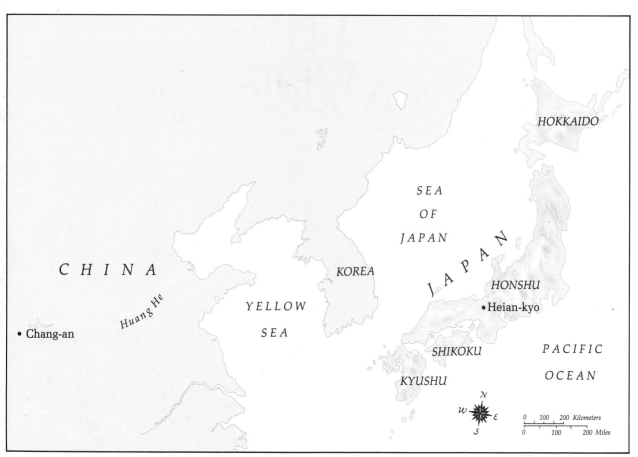

MAP EXERCISE

Chinese religious beliefs and culture found their way to Japan. Use the map to answer the following questions:

1. Which part of the world is shown on this map? Use the world map, page 214, to help you.

2. How far is Japan from China?

3. If a scholar were to leave his home in Heian-kyo and travel to Chang-an to study, how far would he have to travel? What great body of water would he have to cross?

14
Japan's Middle Ages

The story of Japan in its middle ages, from 795 to 1185, has two separate parts. One part takes place in Heian-kyo (HAY-yuhn-kee-OH), where the emperor moved the capital in 794. The city's name, which means "Capital of Peace and Tranquility," suited the way of life of its well-to-do residents. The other part of the story takes place far away, in the wilder countryside, where great landowners and clan leaders ruled the land.

A Code of Conduct. In the new capital, the emperor lost his power to the Fujiwara family in 858. The Fujiwara ruled Japan for about 300 years. Under their rule, the nobles and their families enjoyed a life of luxury. They created a culture of grace and beauty which took some ideas from China, yet was uniquely Japanese.

Heian-kyo, which poets called the "City of Purple Hills and Crystal Streams," was near forested hills and mountains with lakes, streams, and waterfalls. The nobles had large homes with beautiful gardens. A typical garden had its own lake with carefully placed rocks and an island with pine trees on it. The ground was covered with white sand to reflect moonlight.

The well to do and members of the court followed a complex social code which set forth how people were expected to look and behave. Both men and women spent a lot of time with their clothing and makeup. They blackened

This detail from a screen painting shows women enjoying themselves in the dance of the Cherry Blossom Festival.

their teeth, since white teeth were considered ugly, and powdered their faces white. Women plucked their eyebrows and painted false ones high on their foreheads.

The code also told people what perfume they should wear for each occasion. It required that a romance be started by sending a short poem written on special paper. If the would-be lover enclosed a flower, it had to be a certain color.

We know these details of court life because they were recorded by the two most important writers of the period—Lady Murasaki Shikibu (moor-ah-SAH-kee she-KEE-boo) and Lady Sei Sonagan (say SHUN-ah-gahn).

Lady Murasaki wrote one of the world's first great novels, *The Tale of the Genji* (gahn-shee). Written in about the year 1000, it tells the story of the life and loves of Prince Genji, or the "Shining Prince." It is a huge work, 4,234 pages in length. The novel tells how the upper class behaved and how it felt about politics and religion. It also describes how the people strove for beauty in all parts of their lives. In the following edited passage, Lady Murasaki shows just how far they carried this "cult of beauty." She is describing the upper-class women who served the Fujiwara ruler:

> On that day all the ladies who waited on His Majesty had taken particular care with their dress. One of them, however, had made a small error in matching the colors at the opening of her sleeves. When she approached His Majesty to put something

in order, the High Court Nobles noticed the mistake and stared at her. This was a source of lively regret to Lady Shaishō (sye-sho) and the others. It was really not such a serious mistake; only the color of one of the robes was a shade too pale at the opening.

The Way of the Warrior. While the city dwellers were following their code, something very different was going on in the countryside. Great landowners and clan leaders had created large estates. More and more, they ruled these estates according to their own laws, rather than the emperor's laws. Small farmers gave their land to these "lords" and paid taxes to them instead of to the government in Heian-kyo. In return, the farmers received protection.

Why did the small farmers need to be protected? The great lords, called *daimyo* (DYM-yoh), which means "great names," hired lesser lords to fight for them. These warriors were called *samurai* (sahm-uh-RYE) or *bushi* (BOO-shee), which meant "one who serves." The great lords often quarreled with each other and the samurai went to battle. The system was much like that of medieval Europe with its lords and knights.

A samurai warrior was fiercely loyal to his lord, ready to lay down his life, if necessary. He followed his own code of behavior, which came to be called *bushido* (boo-SHEE-doh), or "way of the warrior." The samurai code stressed having a strong body and mind. It said that the warrior's job was to fight and kill his

Yoritomo Minimoto became shogun in the eleventh century. He created a system of government that lasted for 800 years.

lord's enemies. He would do this on horseback, with bows and arrows. Long steel swords became popular later on.

If a samurai's courage failed him, he lost his honor. But the samurai could get back his honor by taking his own life in a ritual called *seppuku* (seh-POO-koo).

Rise of the Shoguns. Samurai warriors were important players in the story of Japan up to modern times. Their first great role was in a twelfth century battle between two clans, the Taira (TY-rah) and the Minamoto (mih-nuh-MOH-toe). The two families fought for control of the royal court after the Fujiwara family lost their power.

The Minamoto family won the battle and a military leader named Yoritomo be-

came *shogun* (SHOH-gun), or "a general who defeats barbarians."

Yoritomo developed a system of government that remained in place for almost 800 years, until 1868. The shogun ruled the daimyo and their samurai in the name of the emperor. But he could appoint ministers, control courts of law, armies, and roads, and collect taxes.

After the Minamoto shoguns lost their power, several other families controlled the government. The shoguns began to encourage more contact with the world outside Japan. Japanese trade expanded greatly during this time.

The Tokugawa shogun had welcomed the Europeans, and traded with them. More and more Europeans began to visit

16th-century picture scroll shows Portuguese traders in Japan looking very foreign in their plaid pants and tall hats.

Japan in the next few decades. Many of them were missionaries, who wanted the Japanese to become Christians.

By the 1590's, the shogun decided that the Europeans, especially the missionaries, were a threat to his government. He began a program to keep Japan free from outside influences. Almost all trade with Europe was ended. All Europeans were thrown out of Japan. Trade with China and other Asian countries was restricted. The Japanese people could not travel outside Japan. This was called a *policy of isolation*. Under this policy, Japan became isolated from the rest of the world. It stayed that way until modern times.

✎ Quick Check

1. *Describe the code of conduct followed by upper-class city dwellers. How do we know about the culture of upper-class Japanese in early times?*

2. *Compare life in the city with life in the countryside. Who ruled the countryside? How did these rulers retain their power?*

3. *Who were the samurai? What was the "way of the warrior"?*

4. *Who were the shoguns? How did they come to power? Why were they able to maintain power?*

5. *Describe Japan's policy of isolation. When did it begin? Why did Japan's rulers isolate Japan from the outside world?*

98

15
Three Great Dynasties: Yuan, Ming, and Ching

North of China lay vast plains. In summer the plains were hot and dry. In winter they were cold and windy. Such plains were not good for farming. But they were perfect for grazing horses, sheeps, goats, and other animals.

The people who lived on those northern plains were mainly nomads. With their herds, the nomads wandered from place to place. These people could stand cold, hunger, and thirst. They could ride their horses long distances. Sometimes their only food was mare's milk.

The Mongol Conquest. The fiercest of the nomads were the Mongols (MAHN-golz). Actually, the Mongols were not one group but a collection of tribes speaking related languages. By 1206, one Mongol tribe had managed to unite most of the others under its leadership. The chief of that powerful tribe took the title of Genghis Khan (GENG-gis kahn). That meant "Ruler of the World."

For Genghis Khan, the main joy in life was conquest. Between 1206 and 1227, he took control of northern China. Before he had finished, his empire stretched from eastern Europe to Korea. It was one of the largest empires the world has seen.

Genghis Khan's great weapon was warriors on horseback who were armed with bows and arrows. One of their methods was the surprise attack. They would storm the enemy and let their arrows fly. Then they would ride away quickly, before the enemy could strike back. The rumor that a Mongol army was near struck terror into people's hearts.

Genghis Khan's grandson was Kublai

Mongolian warriors were expert at hitting their targets from the saddle. Ghengis Kahn (below), founded Mongol empire.

(KOO-blie) Khan. He inherited the Mongol empire, including northern China. Within a few years he conquered the rest of China. In 1297 Kublai Khan took the Chinese throne, becoming the first "barbarian" emperor. He began what was called the Yuan (YOO-ahn) dynasty (1279-1368).

Kublai Khan appointed many Mongols to high positions. But he kept Chinese officials as well to serve as advisers and helpers. The Chinese were shocked by the rough manners and harsh ways of the Mongols. They felt shame at having to serve such masters.

Kublai Khan, the first foreign emperor of China

In time, the Mongols began to learn Chinese ways. But many problems remained in their relations with the people they had conquered. One of the biggest was language. Few of the Mongols spoke Chinese, and even fewer Chinese spoke the language of the Mongols. Mongol rulers had to use translators just to talk to their advisers.

However, the Mongol rulers did help China in many ways. For example, they opened China to many new outside influences. Travelers and traders, such as Marco Polo from Venice in Italy, made their way to the new Chinese capital Khanbalik (kon-buh-LEEK). Muslims from the west visited China too. They won many converts in western China. In that part of China, the Muslim faith re-mains strong to this day.

From contacts with the Chinese, Mongol leaders learned about gunpowder. Armed with their new discovery, they tried to invade Japan. But a great ·wind destroyed the Mongol fleet at sea. Not until the nineteenth century would foreign fleets again menace Japan.

The Ming Dynasty. The Mongols ruled China for less than a century. Then they began to quarrel among themselves. Floods and famines made the Chinese people rebel. Finally, Chinese leaders formed armies to drive out the Mongols.

In 1368, the Mongols went back to their northern plains. The leader of one of the Chinese armies, Hung-Wu (hoong-woo), occupied Khanbalik and named himself emperor. He began the Ming or "brilliant" dynasty (1368-1644).

Hung-Wu moved the capital south to Nanjing (nan-JING). Nanjing means "southern capital." He then set about restoring China's economy, which had grown weak under the last Mongol emperors. He encouraged peasants to cultivate ruined land by lowering their taxes. He even set up programs for rebuilding dams and planting trees.

Hung-Wu's son, Yung-lo (yoong-low), moved the capital back to the site of Khanbalik. There, on top of the old city, he built a new city that he called Beijing (bay-JING). Beijing means "northern capital." Except for the years 1928 to 1949, Beijing has been China's capital ever since.

At the center of Beijing was the great

A marble bridge over the River of Gold leads to the Forbidden City. At the heart of this complex of gardens, lakes, and palaces, is the imperial throne.

royal palace, which was called the Forbidden City. The plan of the city of Beijing matched Yung-lo's view of the world: the Forbidden City was the center of Beijing; Beijing was the ruling center of China; and China was the "Central Country" of the world.

One of the first things Yung-lo wanted to do was to explore lands beyond his empire. He sent fleets of ships to Southeast Asia and beyond. Some of the ships were very large—as much as 400 feet in length. That was almost four times longer than the longest ship used by Columbus in 1492.

In 1405 one of Yung-lo's admirals set out with 52 ships. His crew numbered an astonishing 28,000 men. Using sea charts and the magnetic compass, the fleet visited what are now Sri Lanka and India. A later fleet sailed as far as the east coast of Africa.

The Chinese traded their goods at many of these places. One of their most prized exports was *porcelain* (POHR-cuh-luhn). This was a type of fine white clay mixture that became very hard and strong when it was heated to a high temperature. Ming artisans made dishes, vases, and decorative objects out of porcelain. The blue and white porcelains of this period are famous and are displayed in museums around the world.

The Ming dynasty lasted almost 300 years. Toward the end of Ming rule, Christian missionaries from Europe traveled to China. Many of those missionaries belonged to the Jesuit (JEZH-uh-wuht) order of the Roman Catholic church. The Jesuits introduced Chinese leaders to the science and technology of Europe. But they won only a few converts to Christianity.

Manchus Take Over. The Ming dynasty finally began to weaken. Rebellions broke out, then finally civil war. Some Chinese rebels asked for help from a group of warrior nomads from the northeast. These nomads were the Manchus (MAN-chooz) from the province of Manchuria (man-CHUR-ee-uh). They were distant cousins of the Mongols.

After helping to settle the civil war, the Manchus refused to leave. Instead, they captured Beijing. Then they conquered all of China. Once again, the Chinese would be forced to live under foreign rule.

The Manchus ruled China from 1644 to 1911. Their dynasty is known as the Ching. Like the Mongols, the Manchus needed the Chinese to help run the government. They appointed both Manchu and Chinese officials.

The Manchus did not want to become too much like the Chinese. They were afraid that if they got too friendly, the Chinese would have a chance to rebel. So the emperor declared that Manchus and Chinese could not marry each other. And, as a sign of Manchu power, he ordered all Chinese men to wear their hair in a *queue* (kyoo). A Chinese man had to braid his hair down the back in a long tail. Then he shaved the rest of his head. This showed that he was loyal to the Manchu ruler.

The Manchu dynasty produced some very good emperors. One of the most famous was Kang-hsi (kahng-shee). He ruled for 61 years, from 1661 to 1722. Kang-hsi expanded China's empire to include Tibet and the island of Taiwan (ty-WAHN). A writer himself, Kang-hsi hired scholars to write encyclopedias and other important books.

The Shadow of Europe. During the Manchu dynasty, contacts between China and Europe increased. Europeans began to read translations of the Chinese classics. They bought Chinese products like silk. The Chinese, in turn, borrowed European ideas. The Europeans had by now taken the lead in technology. From the Europeans, the Chinese adopted firearms. They modernized the Chinese calendar. They learned new techniques in mathematics and astronomy.

As trade expanded, European nations sought trading posts in China. The Chinese tried to limit foreign traders to a few specific areas. Portugal had begun a colony at Macao (muh-COW), on China's south coast, in 1557. The Manchu emperors accepted gifts from the Portuguese as payment for the right of settlement. The

K'ang-Hsi had great personal charm and wisdom in governing the empire. During his long reign, he was able to subdue Chinese and Mongol uprisings against Manchu rule.

British and other Europeans did most of their trade through the Chinese port of Guangzhou (Canton).

But not all contacts were peaceful. By the nineteenth century, foreign nations were more aggressive. They used military force, or the threat of force, to impose their wishes on China. Japan was not spared either. Soon both the Manchu dynasty and the Japanese shoguns were weakened by foreign powers.

✎ **Quick Check**

1. *Why were the Mongols widely feared?*

2. *How did the Mongol and Manchu methods of ruling China compare?*

3. *What were some accomplishments of the Ming dynasty?*

4. *How did the Manchus come to rule China?*

5. *What part did Macao and Guangzhou play in the contacts between China and Europe?*

FOREIGN RULERS OF CHINA

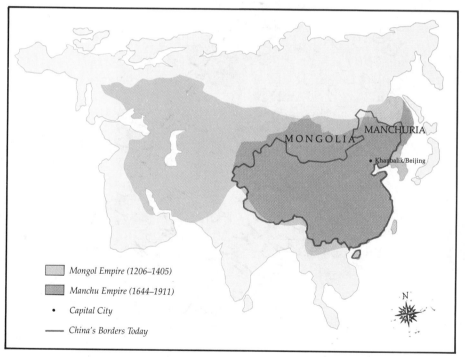

MANCHURIA

MONGOLIA

• Khanbalik/Beijing

☐ Mongol Empire (1206–1405)

☐ Manchu Empire (1644–1911)

• Capital City

—— China's Borders Today

N

Nomadic warriors from Manchuria and Mongolia ruled China for hundred of years. Use the map to answer the following questions:

1. The Great Wall was built to keep invaders out of China. From which direction did the Mongols come?

2. From which direction did the Manchus come?

PART 3
Review and Skills Exercises

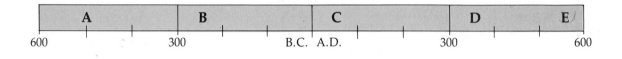

| A | B | C | D | E |

600   300   B.C. | A.D.   300   600

Putting Events in Order

You have read in Parts 1, 2, and 3 about the religion of Buddhism and how it spread in Asia. On the time line above, letters are placed on the approximate dates when certain important events took place. Below is a list. The events are not in order. Decide which event belongs with each letter. Write the letters on a sheet of paper. By each letter write the description of the correct event. Use the index at the back of this book to look up Buddhism if you are unsure of when an event took place.

- King sends Buddhist writings to Japanese Emperor
- Indian Prince finds path to Nirvana
- Emperor Asoka converts to Buddhism
- Buddhism reaches Korea
- Buddhism takes hold in China

Analyzing a Source

You know from your reading that people who study early civilization and cultures have to piece together bits of information. One good source for information about a people is their myths and legends. The passage that follows is from a Japanese legend. It was written in 712 A.D. by a Japanese writer. The Ainu he writes about were living in Japan when the ancestors of today's Japanese people came to the islands. From it we can learn about the Ainu people and the Japanese people. Read the passage carefully and answer the questions that follow.

When our august [highly respected] ancestors descended from heaven in a boat, they found upon this island several barbarous [uncivilized] races, the fiercest of whom were the Ainu.

106

1. What part of the legend tells of a Japanese belief?

2. Part of the legend is a mystery. The Ainu today have been known as a peaceful people for centuries. Why do you think the legend calls them a fierce people?

3. What part of the legend is probably true?

Building Vocabulary Using Social Studies Terms

Read the passage below. Write the numbers 1-8 on a sheet of paper. Match each numbered word or term in the passage with one of the definitions that follow. You may use your textbook, an encyclopedia, and a dictionary to check your choices.

(1)*Archaeologists* agree with the Japanese legend. They have pieced together information about early inhabitants of Japan. They have found (2)*artifacts* such as knife blades, arrowheads, and pottery figures. They know that these artifacts were made by people during the (3)*Neolithic period*. These early people are called the (4)*Jomon*. Some archaeologists believe that the Ainu are (5)*descendants* of the Jomans. They point out some similarities between the way the Jomon and the Ainu did things. The Jomon and the Ainu built huts over shallow pits in the same way. The Ainu put designs on pottery that are similar to designs used by the Jomon.

However, archeologists are not absolutely sure about when and where the Ainu came from. Why are the Ainu a mystery? One reason is that they are different from the Japanese. The Ainu are lighter skinned than the Japanese. They belong to the (6)*Caucasoid* group of people and the Japanese belong to the (7)*Mongoloid* group. These groups have physical differences that tell scientists that the two peoples came from different places.

There are other mysteries about the Ainu. Their language is not related to any other language. The Ainu had no writing. These factors make it difficult to connect the Ainu with other early peoples.

Today a small number of Ainu—about 14,000—remain. They live in villages in northern Japan. We don't know why the early Japanese thought the Ainu were fierce. They have been known as peaceful for centuries. Today the Ainu are a (8)*remnant culture*—an ancient people.

a. a group of people that includes some Asians and Europeans

b. a group of people that includes the Chinese and Japanese

c. scientists who study the remains of early people and communities

d. a period of time also known as the stone age

e. an ancient culture of Japan

f. a small surviving part of a culture

g. tools, utensils, and art of a group of people

h. came from, or related to

PART
4

PRE-COLUMBIAN AMERICA

About 20,000 years ago—or perhaps more—small groups of people from Asia found their way to what is now Alaska. How did they do this? A stretch of icy water—the Bering (BAIR-ing) Strait—separates Asia from present-day Alaska. The distance is about 50 miles, not counting some islands in the middle. Did people sail there? Did they paddle boats?

Some people may have come in such ways. Others, however, probably *walked* from Asia to North America. The Bering Strait today is rather shallow. If the sea level were to drop lower, some of the sea bottom would become dry land. Then a land bridge would link Asia to the North American Continent.

That is what happened during several periods known as Ice Ages. During those times the earth's climate cooled. Huge sheets of ice formed on land. That ice did not melt in the summer and flow out to sea. It just kept getting thicker. Year after year, rain and snow fell on the ice. The rain froze solid. More and more water became locked in ice. As a result, the level of the oceans dropped. During one or more of those Ice Ages, people from Asia crossed into the Americas.

Over many generations, groups of these first Americans grew and divided into more groups. They spread out across North America. Some groups moved south, to Central America. Others went even farther, to South America.

They settled in woodlands and in deserts, in valleys and on plains. They made their homes in cold places and in hot places. Each group developed a *culture*, or way of life, that was suited to its own special surroundings.

Remember that these developments took place over many generations, and over many centuries. As time passed, many groups lost touch with others that had been neighbors or close relatives. New ways of living led to the introduction of new words in the people's speech. In time, more than 1,000 separate languages developed. Each group had its own language and its own culture. Some of the cultures were quite complex.

Europeans "Discover" America. All this took place in the Americas before 1492 A.D. People in Europe, Asia, and Africa knew nothing about such events.

Page 108: Mayan temples at Tikal in the Guatemala jungle.

110

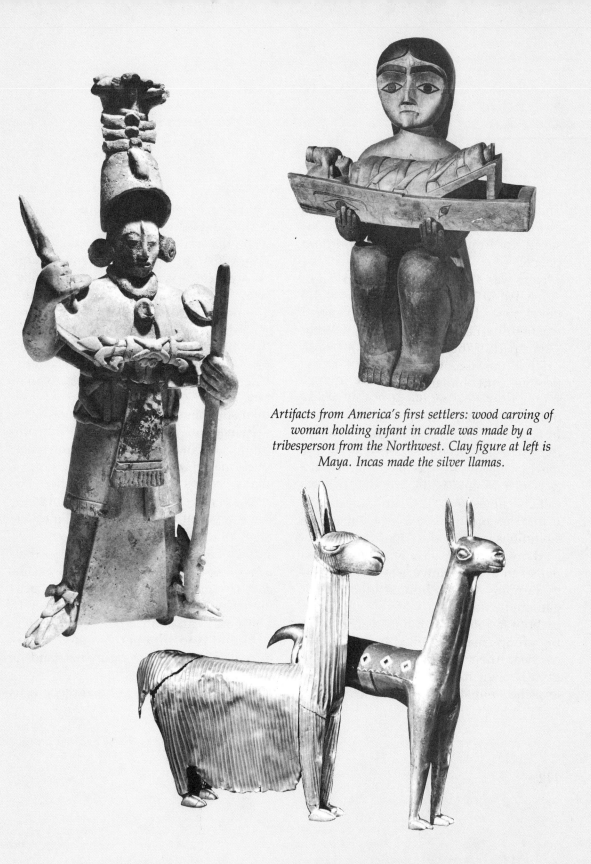

Artifacts from America's first settlers: wood carving of woman holding infant in cradle was made by a tribesperson from the Northwest. Clay figure at left is Maya. Incas made the silver llamas.

That is why it came as a big surprise to Europeans when Christopher Columbus sailed to America in 1492 and found people.

Here was an unknown land, an entire "New World." But Columbus himself did not know that. He thought he had reached the East Indies, off the coast of Asia—part of the "Old World." Because of that mistake, Columbus called the people he met Indians.

Of course, the people of the Americas did not think of themselves as "Indians." In fact, each group had its own name in its own language. Often, the name meant simply "the people." Today, we call such groups native Americans. We call the times they lived in pre-Columbian. This means that they lived before Columbus came to the Americas.

Many Groups, Many Differences. Some groups of native Americans lived by farming. Others hunted or fished or gathered wild foods. Many groups lived by both farming and hunting. The farming groups usually settled in villages, to be near their crops. But the hunting groups often moved their homes to follow the animals. That is, many of the hunting groups were nomadic, or wandering peoples.

The differences went far beyond how the groups got their food. Some groups were peaceful, and some were warlike. Some were ruled by powerful individuals. Some were ruled by groups of elders, or older leaders. Others had developed a form of democracy in which both men and women helped to make decisions.

Bending to Nature's Ways. Native Americans did not think of themselves as one people, and indeed they were many different peoples. But almost all the groups had one thing in common. They thought of themselves as being a part of nature.

The native American people did not have modern tools and machines. It seemed to them that people could not and should not control nature. So they learned to live with nature as it was. Today, modern technology has given people other ideas. Modern societies seem to think they can control nature. If there is a piece of land with nothing on it, someone usually wants to farm that land or build on it.

Native Americans regarded the land as

16
The Mayas: Keeping Time with the Gods

You are cutting your way through a tropical forest. Suddenly the tree trunks and vines give way to a small clearing. Giant stone ruins tower over the clearing. You have stumbled upon an ancient Maya (MY-uh) temple-city, somewhere in the Yucatan (yoo-kah-TAHN), in southeastern Mexico. The stone has crumbled in places, but tall pillars and huge buildings remain. Strange stone faces peer out from the pillars and the walls. Are the faces humans? Snakes? Creatures that are part human and part beast? Who built this place? What was it like in its glory?

Archaeologists think they know. They have studied more than 130 Maya temple-cities scattered through parts of Mexico, Guatemala, Honduras, and Belize.

They have learned many facts about the Mayas' civilization. This civilization was at its height from about 300 to 900 A.D. Then it suddenly declined.

Culture of the Mayas. The Mayas are noted for three great achievements. They had a good knowledge of arithmetic and *astronomy*, the study of the stars and the planets. They developed a very precise calendar and a complex system of writing. Modern scientists are still learning how to read Maya writing.

In these ways, the Mayas were more advanced than some other civilizations of their time. Yet, in other ways, the Mayas lagged behind the civilizations of Europe and Asia. They had no wheeled carts nor did they use plows. They did not know how to work metal into knives and tools.

115

They had no way of measuring weight. And they had no large-scale system of government. Instead, they lived in small city-states, which were centered around their elaborate temple-cities. These city-states were constantly at war with one another.

Maya temple-cities were built mainly for religious purposes. They were used for special ceremonies. Many scientists think that they had no full-time residents except for priests. Others argue that the temple-cities housed many thousands of people.

We do know that most of the Mayas were farmers. They grew corn, squash, cotton, and a few root crops. Maya farms were probably scattered around the outskirts of temple-cities. Some Mayas were members of an upper class—a nobility. From this class came kings and queens and the priests who directed Maya religious practices.

Nobles and priests could write and do arithmetic. They also learned astronomy. These skills were used especially for religious ceremonies. For example, Maya priests figured out when eclipses of the sun would occur. They scheduled colorful religious festivals for such dates. To the Mayas, knowing how the sun, moon, and stars moved was a way of knowing the will of the gods.

Let us imagine a Maya temple-city on the day of a festival. We join masses of people in a great open court. Around us are great stone staircases leading to higher levels and to several temples. Some of the temples sit atop pyramids. At one side is a ball court where ceremonial games will be played today.

One stairway in particular draws our attention. The facing of each step contains writing in a form of picture symbols, or *hieroglyphs*. Here and there along the stairway are statues of human figures.

Around us we see more statues and sculptures. Some show people. Others picture two-headed dragons and other creatures. Tall pillars are spotted about the open spaces. On the front and back, human figures are carved. On the sides appear writings in Maya hieroglyphs. Today the priests will dedicate a new pillar, or *stele* (STEE-lee). It will mark the end of a 20-year period of the Maya calendar.

We see many priests, each wearing a huge headdress. The head gear contains dozens of bright blue-green feathers. The feathers are from the tropical bird called the quetzal (keht-SAHL). Otherwise the priests are dressed much like the other men. They are bare-chested, with breech-cloths or skirts over their lower body. Women, too, wear only light clothing. Of course, we are in a place that is warm all year.

Not all the events at this festival are happy. By our standards, some of the religious ceremonies are shocking. The Mayas believe that their deities must be "fed" every day with human blood.

Close-up of Maya stone carving with seated figure in foreground

Carved stone medallion with figure of Maya ballgame player in center

Kings, queens, and nobles all cut themselves regularly and offer their blood as a sacrifice. They believe that this will bring them closer to their deities. They also want to experience the "visions" that can sometimes come with a great loss of blood.

Today the queen is making a sacrifice. She cuts her tongue and lets the blood flow on a special cloth. The cloth is then burned. The Mayas believe the deities can only "eat" the sacrifice if it is burned.

Later in the day there will be more sacrifices. There is a war being fought between this city-state and another one. Five prisoners of war were captured a month ago. For the past month, they have suffered while priests drew blood from them. Today these prisoners will play a game of ball. The loser will be killed and his heart offered to feed the deities.

118

We leave the sacrifice and go to look at some of the artwork in the temples. We see pottery that is painted in cheerful colors. We see jewelry made of precious green jade engraved with human and animal designs. Materials such as jade are not native to the immediate area. The local Mayas get such objects by trading with people who live in mountains to the south and east. They also trade for a black rock called *obsidian* (uhb-SIHD-ee-uhn), or volcano-glass. Obsidian is very important to the Mayas. It can be chipped to make a sharp edge for hoes and knives.

Now people are forming into a line. Some are putting on animal masks that represent the faces of deities. We pick up a rattle made from a squash gourd, and take our place in line. The procession begins, to the sound of trumpets and drums and turtle-shell noisemakers. We add to the music by shaking our rattle.

Festival days were a break in the Maya routine. Most people had to work in the fields on ordinary days. Or they did work on the great temples. Millions of baskets of earth had to be carried by hand. They were dumped in a pile to form the base for this temple-city. Then great rocks had to be cut and moved into place. The Mayas had no carts or animals to help carry the great stones. People pulled or carried it all. Building a Maya temple was a task that took longer than any one person's lifetime.

Priests directed every step in the process. They worked out the proper po-sition for each building. They made sure that the stars, planets, moon, and sun would cast their light in the correct parts of the temples at exact times of the year.

The decline of the Maya civilization came quite suddenly. Around the year 900, the Mayas abandoned one temple-city after another. Did warriors from other groups conquer the Mayas? Did Maya farmers revolt against the priests and nobles? Was there a natural disaster such as a flood or earthquake? Perhaps we will never know. When Spanish soldiers arrived in the 1500's, they found only scattered settlements of Mayas. Trees and weeds had already swallowed up many of the temple-cities.

Some two million people of Maya descent live in Mexico and Central America today. Many speak the Maya language, or related native American languages. Most are Roman Catholics now. However, some people still practice certain ancient Maya rituals. The past lives on.

✎ Quick Check

1. *In what part of the Americas did the Mayas live?*

2. *How did the Mayas' civilization compare with civilizations in other parts of the world at the same time?*

3. *What purpose might the Mayas have had in putting up a stele?*

4. *Into what main groups was Maya society divided?*

5. *When and why did Maya civilization decline?*

17
The Aztecs:
Island in a Lake

The Mayas were one of several groups that built complex cultures in Central America. Another center of civilization lay to the north. Called the Olmec (OHL-mehk) culture, it was in what is now central Mexico.

The Olmec culture began in that area as early as 1500 B.C. The Mayas borrowed some ideas from the Olmecs. They built massive stone heads and temples. But the Olmec culture began to disappear after 400 B.C.

A second culture, known as Teotihuacan (tay-oh-tee-wah-KAHN), began about 100 B.C. Teotihuacan was the name of a city in an area known as the valley of Mexico. Teotihuacan is near present-day Mexico City.

As many as 100,000 people may have lived in Teotihuacan. The people built two large pyramids. They worshiped a feathered serpent-deity that they called Quetzalcoatl (keht-SAHL-kuh-WAH-tul). They raised food on artificial islands in a giant lake. Then came a long dry spell, crop failures, and enemy attacks. Sometime after 600 A.D., Teotihuacan was abandoned.

Finally, a new people, called the Aztecs (AZ-tehks), entered the valley. At first the Aztecs were one group among many. But they were fierce warriors. In time they conquered their neighbors. They grew to become the most powerful people in all of North America before the Europeans came.

Sacrificing to a Deity. The Aztecs followed a harsh religion. Their chief deity, the warlike Huitzilopochtli (wee-tsee-loh-PEHTCH-tlee) was violent. He could use lightning bolts to crush his enemies. He was associated with the sun. In the Aztec religion, the sun represented the forces of good. Night represented the forces of evil.

Each day the deity, like the sun, fought a battle against night. So each day he needed food. This the Aztecs offered—in

the form of human hearts and blood. They sacrificed many people in the name of their religion. But they were not alone in this. The Mayas, and perhaps other native Americans, also practiced human sacrifice (see Chapter 16).

The person to be sacrificed was stretched out on a stone altar. A priest used a stone knife to slice open the victim's chest. Then he ripped out the beating heart. The grim scene was repeated often. When a temple to Huitzilopochtli was built, some 20,000 victims were sacrificed in the ceremony. According to Az-

tec teachings, it was considered an honor to be sacrificed.

To get enough victims, the Aztecs constantly fought wars. They fought and defeated many of their neighbors. The unlucky neighbors then had to give food, cloth, and weapons to the Aztecs. They also had to give them slaves, and victims for the sacrifice. All this helped the Aztecs fight more wars and continue to practice their religion.

The Great Capital. About 1325 A.D., the Aztecs began to build a new city in the valley of Mexico. They called their city

"Map" describing the journey of the Aztecs to the island in a lake which became their capital

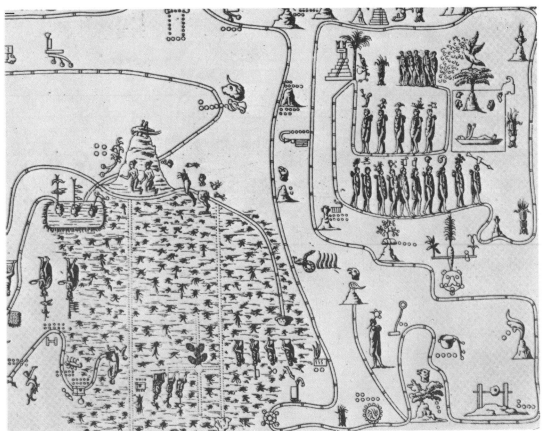

Tenochtitlan (tay-NOCH-tee-TLAHN), which means "cactus from the rock." It grew to be one of the greatest cities of its time. Tenochtitlan had about 300,000 residents at the start of the sixteenth century. In size, it was three times as large as London, England, at the time.

Built on an island in a lake surrounded by mountains, Tenochtitlan was a beautiful city. It had gardens filled with many kinds of fruits and vegetables. Broad canals cut through the city. Boats carried both people and goods from place to place. Flowers grew everywhere. During festivals, the narrow stone streets were filled with music and dancing.

All the canals and roads led to the center of the city. Here stood many flat-topped pyramids. On top of the pyramids were temples.

Around the plaza lay a huge marketplace. Signs marked the marketplace off into sections, one for each trade or product. Shoppers could buy chocolate or feathers, meat or fruit, gold or jewelry, stone blades, and many other items. In one corner slaves were offered for sale. Some of the slaves were held by collars attached to long poles. The slaves included both women and men.

The Spanish Arrive. About 500 Spanish soldiers marched into this city in the year 1519. Leading them was their commander, Hernando Cortés (core-TEZ). He was a Spanish soldier looking for gold. Spaniards had already conquered Cuba, which had little gold. Now Cortés was eager to try his luck in Mexico.

The Aztecs in Tenochtitlan greeted the newcomers with amazement. They had never seen either Europeans or horses. The Spaniards, in turn, were amazed at the beauty and wealth of the Aztec city.

The Aztec emperor, Montezuma (mahn-tuh-ZOO-muh), had already sent messengers to meet the foreigners. He welcomed them and gave them gold and other gifts.

Why was the Aztec ruler so friendly to the Spanish strangers? By strange coincidence, the Spaniards had arrived during a special year in the Aztec religious calendar. According to legend, the serpent-deity Quetzalcoatl would return that year. Quetzalcoatl had been worshiped in the valley of Mexico for hundreds of years, even before Aztec times. This deity was said to have sailed off to the east, promising to return. Now, from the east, came the Spaniards. Had the deity kept its promise and finally returned?

Montezuma could not be sure of the answer. Although he did not entirely trust the Spaniards, he let down his guard. A small Spanish force took Montezuma prisoner. Using the emperor as a spokesperson, Cortés and his soldiers seized control of the capital.

Montezuma tried to keep his people calm. After several months, however, the Aztecs in the city rebelled. They heard that the Spaniards had killed some of their priests and nobles while they were worshiping in a temple. Angry mobs killed Montezuma and drove the Spaniards out of the city.

This Aztec drawing shows the Spanish conquest as the destruction of the Aztec civilization.

The War of Conquest. In the war that followed, Cortés and his soldiers had help. Many native American groups considered the Aztecs their enemies. They were glad to help the Spaniards fight the Aztecs.

The final battle against the Aztecs took place in 1521. Spanish and native American armies controlled the lake. They would not let any food into Tenochtitlan. The Aztecs held out for 85 days. The people suffered from hunger and from smallpox, a disease the Spaniards had brought from Europe. With no natural resistance to the disease, many Aztecs died. Finally, they surrendered. Their days of power and glory were over.

The Spaniards destroyed much of the beautiful city. They tore down the pyramids, temples, and palaces. They used the stones to put up their own buildings. The new city, now called Mexico City, rose on the ruins of the old.

Today the Aztecs are not forgotten. The last Aztec emperor, Cuauhtemoc (kwah-oo-TAY-muhck), is remembered as a symbol of courage for having fought the Spaniards to the bitter end. Aztec ruins still stand in Mexico City alongside Spanish and modern-day buildings. Many Mexicans are descendants of the Aztecs and speak a modern version of the Aztec language. Many Aztec words have entered the Spanish and English languages. Words such as *chocolate, tomato, coyote, chili*, and *avocado* come from the Aztec language.

✎ Quick Check

1. *What special site did the Aztecs choose for their capital?*

2. *Describe the reasoning behind the Aztecs' use of human sacrifice.*

3. *Where did the Aztecs build their temples?*

4. *Why did Montezuma greet the Spaniards as he did?*

5. *What happened to Montezuma and Tenochtitlan?*

MAYA AND AZTEC CIVILIZATIONS

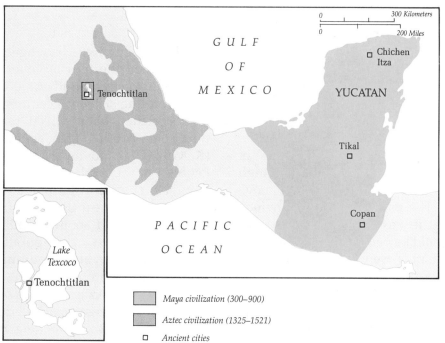

Maya civilization (300–900)

Aztec civilization (1325–1521)

□ Ancient cities

In what is now central and southeastern Mexico, several complex cultures developed. Use the map to answer the following questions:

1. What part of the world is shown on this map? Use the world map, page 214, to help you.

2. What body of water surrounded the city of Tenochtitlan?

3. Which civilization occupied the Yucatan?

4. Which civilization is older, the Maya or the Aztec?

18
The Incas:
Kingdom of the Sun

The messenger ran up the steep mountain path. When he glanced downward, he knew he was high above the clouds. Snowy mountain peaks lay on either side, poking into the blue sky above the clouds.

Why wasn't the messenger out of breath? How could he stand such high altitudes—more than 10,000 feet above sea level? The air was thin there, which meant that it was low in oxygen. Most people would be panting. They might become faint after even a brief walk on the mountain paths.

The messenger, though, was used to such heights. His people had lived for many years in the thin air. Their efficient lungs and strong hearts allowed them to live comfortably amid the clouds. Who were these mountain Americans? They were a group we call the *Inca* (IHN-kah). In their language, Inca means "the king."

The Inca Empire. Messengers such as these helped the Inca to govern a huge empire in western South America. At its largest, in the sixteenth century, the empire stretched about 3,000 miles from north to south. The capital—Cuzco (KOOS-koh)—and much of the empire lay high in the Andes (AN-deez) Mountains. No empire in Europe at that time was anywhere near as large. In all, the empire contained about six million people. By contrast, the population of England was then about four million.

The Inca empire developed about the same time the Aztecs were conquering Mexico. It was most powerful during the period 1438-1493. But a long period of earlier native American development paved the way for the Inca empire.

Native Americans living near the west coast of South America had begun to build temples as early as 2500 B.C. Before

126

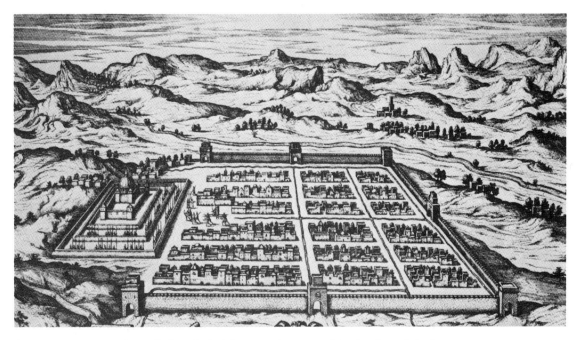

The walled capital of Cuzco as it appeared in the time of the Incas

1800 B.C. they had built the first pyramids in the Americas. They began to mine gold and copper. They learned to heat and blend different metals to make strong weapons. At different times they may have traded with the peoples of Central America.

Many different groups have lived in the Andes since 2500 B.C. The Inca managed to bring dozens of these groups under one system of government.

To tie this huge empire together, workers built many roads. Four great highways fanned out from Cuzco. From these, more roads branched out across mountains, forests, and deserts. They reached into every part of the empire. Workers paved the roads with large, flat stones. They built swaying rope bridges over deep canyons.

Daily Life. The Inca way of life was smooth and orderly. They believed in strong discipline. This was good in some ways, but bad in others. Their people had plenty to eat, and warm clothes to wear. But they had almost no rights or freedoms as we know them. They even had to get permission from the government to travel from one village to another.

Like the Aztecs, the Incas were expert fighters. They attacked and conquered many of their neighbors. But the Incas did not always have to fight. Some groups surrendered peacefully. They had heard that the Incas treated their subjects fairly and would bring peace and prosperity. That was usually true.

The Incas had a sort of "foreign-aid program" for people they had taken over. Sometimes the conquered people had no knowledge of farming. In that case, the Incas sent advisers to their new subjects. The advisers taught them how to build hillside terraces, how to plant, and how to harvest. They even gave them seeds for the first crops. In this manner, the Incas improved the lives of their subjects. They also improved their own. Now the conquered peoples could grow food that they would share with the Inca noblility.

The Incas had a complex religion centered around their king. They considered the king to be a descendant of the sun deity. In each new territory, the Incas built new temples to the sun deity. But they allowed subject peoples to keep their own deities as well.

Inca Accomplishments. The Incas required all of their subjects to learn the Quechua (KEH-chwah) language. They even had a sort of college that young nobles could attend. However, the Incas had no real system of writing. That is why runners had to memorize the messages they carried.

The Incas did have a method of counting and keeping records. They did so by tying knots in strings that were collected in bunches. A bunch of strings was called a *quipu* (KEE-poo). One string of the quipu was for single numbers, one string for tens, one string for hundreds, and so on. Using quipus, the Incas recorded the empire's population. They also used quipus to keep track of grain storage, and to collect taxes in the form of food.

Inca builders were highly skilled. They put up huge stone buildings without any mortar. Each stone had to be cut by hand. When cut, the stones fit together so closely that not even a modern razor blade could slip between them. Often the stones were covered with a layer of gold or silver from the Incas' rich mines. The fanciest buildings were in Cuzco, the capital. The mountain fortress of Machu Picchu (MAH-choo PEE-choo), 50 miles from Cuzco, was also impressive.

Rise and Fall of the Inca Empire. Two great rulers helped to expand the Inca empire. The first was named Pachacutec (patch-ah-KOO-tehk). The second was his son, Topa (TOH-puh) Inca. After Topa Inca died, the Inca government became weak. Soon arguments led to a civil war.

It was just at this time that Spanish soldiers invaded the empire. Juan Pizarro (hwan puh-ZAHR-oh), the Spanish commander, took the king hostage. This king, Atahuallpa (ah-tah-WAHL-puh), was Topa Inca's grandson. To buy his freedom, Atahuallpa offered to send for gold and silver from every part of the empire. He promised to fill three large rooms with the treasure if Pizarro would agree to free him. Atahuallpa's people

THE INCAS EXPAND

COLOMBIA

ECUADOR

Amazon River

PERU

MACCHU PICCHU
▲•Cuzco

PACIFIC

OCEAN

BRAZIL

BOLIVIA

Inca empire in the time of:

Pachacutec (1438-1463)

Pachacutec and Topa Inca (1463-1471)

Topa Inca (1471-1493)

Huayna Capac (1493-1525)

• Capital city

------- Modern bounderies

PARAGUAY

CHILE

ATLANTIC

OCEAN

N

URUGUAY

ARGENTINA

0   600 Kilometers

0   400 Miles

At its greatest extent, the Inca empire stretched 3,000 miles north to south. Use the map to answer the following questions:

1. What part of the world is shown on this map. Use the world map, page 214, to help you.

2. Which ruler gained the most land for the Inca empire?

3. In which modern countries was the Inca empire located?

The baths at Sacsahuaman, the Inca fortress just north of Cuzco, Peru, still stand today.

paid the ransom. But Pizarro did not keep his part of the bargain. He ordered the king strangled.

The Spaniards then took over the Inca empire. They made it part of a huge Spanish colony in the New World. Today little remains of the Inca empire but the majestic ruins of fortresses and temples. There are also people who are the descendants of the Incas and their subjects. Millions of Peruvians, Ecuadorians, and Bolivians still speak the Incas' ancient Quechua language with pride.

✎ **Quick Check**

1. *Where and when did the Inca empire flourish?*

2. *Why were Inca messengers able to run even at high altitudes?*

3. *How did the Incas treat the people over whom they ruled?*

4. *Without writing, how did the Incas keep records?*

5. *Describe the building techniques of the Incas.*

130

19
The Anasazi:
Living on Many Levels

Come forth from wherever you live,
Little wind-blown clouds.
Thin, wispy clouds,
Filled with living waters,
Stay with us.

The poem above is a plea for rain. It was written by a people who lived in one of the driest parts of the Americas. Today that area is in the U.S. Southwest, and includes New Mexico, Arizona, Utah, and Colorado.

The earliest groups in the area lived by hunting and gathering food. By 100 A.D., these people had learned to farm. They raised crops of corn, squash, and kidney beans and grew cotton. They began to build permanent villages. The Anasazi (ahn-uh-SAH-zee) were one of the most important groups who lived in this area.

Living In A Dry Land The Anasazi were one of the most skillful of all early American groups. They had to be clever to live as farmers in a land with very little rain. They made use of every drop of water they could get. First they placed their fields in areas where streams overflowed during the brief rainy season. Then they dug canals from the streams to their crops. When rains swelled the streams, water overflowed into the canals. This irrigated, or watered, the crops.

Near their fields, the Anasazi built villages. At first they borrowed a trick from small desert animals. They lived underground by digging pits. They covered the tops with a roof of sticks and mud. They dug tunnels to provide a way in and out. In such pit houses the Anasazi could stay cool in summer and warm in winter.

131

Anasazi villages were tucked into mountainsides or under cliffs. Such a hillside village was safe from surprise attack and sheltered from the hot sun.

Anasazi "Apartment Houses." Beginning about 750 A.D., the Anasazis moved their homes above ground. They made walls of stone or *adobe* (uh-DOH-bee). Adobe is a mixture of mud and straw that is baked hard by the sun. Some of the new-style villages were built on high, flat plains, called *mesas*. Others were built into the sides of cliffs.

Anasazi villages were like modern apartment complexes. Many structures had several stories. Like steps in a staircase, each story was set back from the one below. To reach a second-floor apartment, the people climbed ladders to the second-story roof. Then they climbed down other ladders into the apartments themselves.

Some of the apartment houses were huge. One had five stories and more than 800 rooms. More than 1,000 people could have lived there. Some of the many rooms in the houses were used for cooking, eating, and sleeping. Other rooms were used for storing food. Each building also held one or more religious rooms. They are called *kivas* (KEE-vuhs).

Following the Traditional Way. Kivas are still used by modern-day native Americans such as the Hopis, Zunis, and Pueblo people.

Kivas have a special meaning for many Hopis who follow the traditional ways. They believe that humans came to this world from an underworld. The route to this world led up through the waters of a lake, then through a hole known as the *sipapu* (sih-PAH-poo). At the center of each kiva, Hopis place a stone-lined pit. The pit is a symbol of the sipapu.

For many Hopis the kivas are a center of religious life. Groups of Hopi men meet in the kivas to carve colorful masks. They wear these in ceremonies that call for rain. The men also make doll-like figures. Both the masks and the dolls represent spirits called *kachinas* (kuh-CHEE-nuhs). The old customs of the Hopi also include worship of sun, earth-mother, and moon deities.

Although men are in charge of religion, women have special responsibilities. Traditional Hopi society is organized by clans. Both men and women belong to the clan of their mother, not of their father.

Traditionally, a Hopi male lives with his wife's family when he marries. He farms land controlled by the women of the clan. Still, he has important responsibilities toward his own mother and sisters. For example, as the uncle of his sister's children, he is responsible for disciplining them. He is also expected to help keep order in his sister's household. Men may also spin and weave cotton into cloth to help clothe the members of their wife's clan.

Today, many Hopis, Zunis, and other Pueblos have moved into cities and lost some of the old traditions. But many others remain in the villages of their ancestors. They still live much as their ancestors did. Their culture is hundreds of years old. It has remained strong to this day.

✎ **Quick Check**

1. *How did the Anasazi people use their land wisely?*

2. *What were the first Anasazi villages like?*

3. *How did later Anasazi villages differ?*

4. *What is the religious significance of the kiva?*

5. *What special role do women play in Hopi life?*

20
The Iroquois: Government by the People

Before Europeans settled there, most of eastern North America was covered by woodlands. Native American groups moved into this region as early as 10,000 B.C. At first they fed themselves by hunting game and gathering wild foods. Then, beginning about 1000 B.C., they learned to make clearings and grow crops. Like many other groups, they grew mostly corn, squash, and beans.

Different woodland groups had different customs. Some built large mounds of earth, which they used as places of burial. Some created earth mounds that were almost as large as the pyramids built elsewhere in the Americas. The mound builders lived from about 1000 B.C. to 700 A.D. They were the ancestors of later groups such as the Iroquois (IHR-uh-kwoy).

A Powerful Group of Tribes. When English settlers arrived in North America in the seventeenth century, the Iroquois were the most powerful native American group they met. Most of the Iroquois made their home in what is now northern New York. A few lived in parts of Pennsylvania and Ohio. Still others lived in Canada.

The Iroquois were not members of a single group. They belonged to different groups that spoke the Iroquois language. Five groups banded together into the Iroquois League in 1570. Those groups were the Mohawk (MOE-hawk), Cayuga (kay-YOO-guh), Oneida (oh-NI-duh), Seneca (SEN-uh-kuh), and Onondaga (ah-nun-DAH-guh). In 1722 a sixth group, the Tuscarora (tuss-kuh-ROAR-uh), joined.

Among the Iroquois, men were warriors and hunters. But women too could take part in warfare. The Iroquois fought against many of their neighbors. Their league made them stronger than most of their native American enemies, who had no permanent allies.

Daily Life. Iroquois men generally hunted and trapped animals. But women could hunt and trap if they wished. Women did most of the planting and growing of food. They also ran the day-to-day affairs of the home.

Like the Southwest groups, the Iroquois were organized into clans. Each clan consisted of several related families. People belonged to their mother's clan. Women were in charge of the land and had the power to choose the leader, or *sachem* (say-chum). Men were usually sachems. But women too could have that role. The leading woman of the clan, or clan matron, was a powerful figure. She could dismiss a sachem if she thought the sachem wasn't doing a good job. Then she and the women of the clan would pick a new one.

Iroquois families lived together in one-story structures called *longhouses*. Each family had its own room off a central hallway. At mealtime the hallway was a busy place, with the women of each family working over their own cooking fire. By custom, each family cooked for itself. But each family shared a taste of its meal with other families in the longhouse.

The Iroquois League. The groups that joined the Iroquois League had not always been allies. Before 1570 they were sometimes enemies. Two leaders proposed the plan of unity. Several groups thought it was a good idea. But one group, the Onondaga, held back. To encourage the Onondaga to join, other groups agreed that the Onondaga should be the keepers of the council fire. That was an honored role, traditionally held by an important sachem. In addition, all league meetings would take place in Onondaga territory.

In some ways, the Iroquois League resembled a democracy. Each of the member groups, for instance, had its own voice in league affairs. The league controlled relations between the member groups and other native American groups. It did so through the Council of Sachems.

As you read the dialogue below, ask yourself what was most democratic about the Iroquois. How did their government differ from our democracy today?

The time: a summer morning in the late 1500's.

The place: a woodland clearing in the Onondaga section of what is now New York State. In the distance stands an Iroquois longhouse.

The scene: a meeting of the Council of Sachems is about to take place in the longhouse. Two sachems—Hunting Bear and Strong Hand—are traveling there on foot. They meet.

HUNTING BEAR: Is this the way to the Council of Sachems?

STRONG HAND: Yes. The longhouse is near. I am headed there myself. Why not walk along with me?

HUNTING BEAR: Thank you. My name is Hunting Bear. I'm a new sachem from the Seneca.

STRONG HAND: I'm Strong Hand, a Mohawk.

HUNTING BEAR: I've been looking forward to this meeting. It is a great honor to have been chosen.

STRONG HAND: I'm sure you will be a good representative. You will have to be ready to both speak and listen.

HUNTING BEAR: I understand. All five groups agree before the council can take action.

STRONG HAND: Yes. That may seem to be a weakness. Sometimes we talk for hours without reaching agreement. We may have to put off taking any action at all. Yet I believe that this is a good thing in the end. When we finally do reach agreement, we have thoroughly considered our decision. There is no "losing" side.

HUNTING BEAR: It is a good system. But tell me, do the sachems get along well as a rule? I have heard about some grumbling against the Onondaga.

STRONG HAND: Well, some people do think it's unfair that the Onondaga get to be the only keepers of the council fire.

HUNTING BEAR: And we Seneca don't see why the Onondaga should get to have the most sachems on the council. After all, the Seneca are the largest of the five groups. Yet we have the fewest sachems.

STRONG HAND: True, that seems unfair. But does it really matter? We are not here as individuals, but as representatives of our groups. It is the five groups that must agree, not the separate sachems.

HUNTING BEAR: I see your point. Of course, we do not represent only ourselves. We must also consider the wishes of our people. The chiefs, the wise men, and especially the clan matrons, who appointed us to be sachems in the first place.

STRONG HAND: Indeed, we must not forget the clan matrons. My friend Sturdy Tree did not come back with me this time. He lost his position as a sachem because he angered his clan matron and the other women of the clan. They warned him to change his ways. But he ignored them, so they dismissed him and chose another man.

HUNTING BEAR: I'm sure Sturdy Tree was deeply hurt. To be dismissed as a sachem is a great humiliation. A successful sachem must keep the women in mind.

STRONG HAND: Yes. The job calls for both wisdom and tact. But here we are at the longhouse. You'll soon see for yourself exactly what the job requires.

✎ Quick Check

1. *Why were the Iroquois a powerful group?*

2. *Describe the role of women in the Iroquois culture. In what ways were they powerful?*

3. *What was the purpose of the Iroquois League? In what ways was it a democratic organization?*

4. *How was the Iroquois League like our democracy today? How was it different?*

21
The Kwakiutl: Giving It All Away

The feast began early and went on far into the night. Slaves brought out one course after another. They served heaping bowls of berries. They carried out platters piled high with clams. They brought tender bits of clover root, great chunks of seal meat, whole salmon, and many other fish and animals and fruits. Finally, the guests rolled their eyes and said they could not eat another bite. No one could eat so much food.

And that was the whole point. The guests were attending a feast known as a *potlatch* (PAHT-lach). The purpose of a potlatch is to give away huge amounts of food and other goods. The host—the person who gives the feast—gains great honor by being generous. The more he can give away, the more of a "big man" he is considered to be.

This potlatch was being given by a leader of the Kwakiutl (kwah-kee-YOO-tuhl) people. The Kwakiutl are one of several native American groups who lived—and still live—along the northwestern coast of North America. Their home is where Canada and the United States meet along the Pacific coast. They still give potlatches. Other groups in that area also give potlatches.

An Area of Abundance. Native American groups began to settle the Northwest thousands of years ago. They did not become farmers. The rivers and the ocean were full of food. There were large sea animals like whales and seals. There were fish like cod, halibut, herring, and salmon. And shellfish like mussels, oysters, and clams could be gathered with ease.

Many clans gave a potlatch when they put up a totem pole. This one can be seen today in Stanley Park, Vancouver, British Columbia.

Kwakiutl men hunted and fished for large fish. Kwakiutl women were responsible for getting most of the group's other food. They gathered vegetables, roots, and berries in the woods. Most of this food could not be found in the winter. But the Kwakiutl were experts at drying, salting, and smoking food to preserve it. This helped them build up large amounts of *surplus*, or extra, food.

With so much food available, the Kwakiutl could well afford to give large feasts. Not just anybody could give a pot-latch, however. A host had to belong to one of the noble families. Such families had inherited special ranks and privileges. The more closely they were related to the leader, the more noble they were.

Noble Kwakiutl families had their own special symbols. They carved these along the sides of logs. Those carved logs were called *totem* (TOH-tuhm) *poles.* Kwakiutl families stood the poles in front of the large plank houses in which they lived. Birds, animals, and human figures were among the designs on the poles.

139

Let's imagine we are invited to a potlatch. We are back in the early 1700's. This period cannot really be called pre-Columbian, because Columbus visited North America centuries before. But European settlers did not reach the Northwest until around 1770. Before contact with the Europeans, the Kwakiutl followed their old traditions.

Our host is a man we will call Noble Wolf. Not long ago Noble Wolf's father, a leader, died. As the oldest son, Noble Wolf will inherit his father's title. But before he can do so, he must give a potlatch. By showing how generous he is, Noble Wolf will prove that he is worthy of becoming a leader.

For many months, Noble Wolf's entire family has been preparing for the potlatch. Brothers and uncles and cousins, sisters and aunts and children—everyone helped. They dried fish for the feast. They cured the pelts of sea otters and sewed them to make warm fur coats. Out of reeds they wove baskets. Out of cedar bark they made blankets. All of these will be given away at the potlatch.

On fishing trips, Noble Wolf's family

A chief sits behind the blankets he is giving away.

saved a special kind of fish—the "candle-fish." The body of a candlefish is full of oil. The body can be strung on a string called a wick. The wick will then soak up the fish's oil. When lighted, it will burn—like a candle. Candlefish will provide light for the potlatch.

Now we are sitting down to eat. When we can eat no more, the speeches begin. Noble Wolf rises to speak first. He thanks the guests for coming. He tells of his late father's life, and what a great chief he was. He hopes he is worthy to follow in his father's footsteps. Then he talks about his family's special connections. He tells a legend about a wolf that saved the life of a long-ago ancestor. Ever since, the family has carved the face of a wolf on its totem poles.

Other speakers—guests—rise in turn. They praise Noble Wolf in flowery words. They say he has given a potlatch worthy of a great chief. From now on, they say, everyone will look upon Noble Wolf with the respect due a chief.

Before the evening ends, Noble Wolf's slaves pass out the gifts. The fanciest gifts go to the guests with the highest rank. Most people seem pleased with their gifts. But one man is not pleased. He thinks that he has been snubbed—that he received less than he deserved. The man will say nothing now. But later, the village will hear from him. He will give his own potlatch. If he can, he will give away even more than Noble Wolf has given. That will show what a great man he is.

For the Kwakiutl it was the potlatch. For the Iroquois it was the Council of Sachems. Each native American group had its own special ways. Each had its own traditions and legends.

In most of the Americas, native Americans were eventually pushed aside by Europeans and other newcomers. Nowadays, native Americans often live in places that the goverment has set aside for them. Other Americans sometimes ask why native Americans still cling to old customs. Why don't they switch to the customs of modern society?

The answer is a simple one. Many native Americans are fiercely proud of their heritage. They do not want to abandon the old ways. One of them has said:

> You will forgive me if I tell you that my people were Americans for thousands of years before your people were. The question is not how you can Americanize us. It is how we can Americanize you. The first thing we want to teach you is that, in the American way of life, each man has respect for his brother's vision. Because each of us respected his brother's dream, we enjoyed freedom here. . . . We have a hard trail ahead of us, but we are not afraid of hard trails.

✎ Quick Check

1. *What was the purpose of a potlatch?*
2. *How were the Kwakiutl able to afford such lavish feasts?*
3. *What sort of person or family might give a potlatch?*
4. *Describe a totem pole and tell how it was used.*

141

PART 4
Review and Skills Exercises

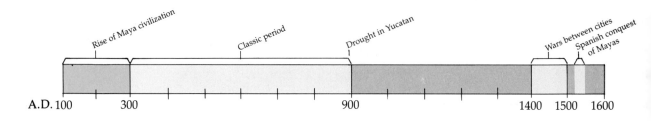

Rise of Maya civilization

Classic period

Drought in Yucatan

Wars between cities

Spanish conquest of Mayas

A.D. 100   300   900   1400 1500 1600

Understanding Events

In Part 4 you read about a number of cultures that developed in the Americas. One of these was the Maya civilization in Central America. Study the time line above and answer the following questions.

1. During the classic period great stone cities were built and the Maya culture spread. How long did this period of history last?

2. What could have caused the Mayas to abandon their cities in the Yucatan at the close of the ninth century?

3. What was happening in Maya society during the rise of the Aztec civilization in the fifteenth century?

4. How old was the Maya civilization when the Spanish appeared?

5. The Maya developed astronomy, and invented writing and the calendar before 300 A.D. During what period of Maya history was this?

6. The fifteenth century marked the fi-

nal decline of Maya civilization. How many centuries was this after the end of the classic period?

Interpreting a Reading

Read the paragraphs below and answer the questions that follow.

A Llama Caravan

During the time of the Inca empire and before, people in the Andes Mountains developed a trading system using the llama, a relative of the camel. Archaeologists have found evidence that caravans of llamas trekked up and down the slopes of the mountains with trade goods as long as 4,000 years ago. People who lived high in the Andes needed grains and other food that could not be grown in their region. They traded goods they did have, such as salt and potatoes, for food grown in the valleys.

Here is what a trek by llama caravan might have been like when Incas ruled a vast empire that stretched across the Andes:

A village near Lake Poopó in what is now Bolivia is a busy place the morning a llama caravan is to leave. Villagers gather around the five llama drovers. The drovers are responsible for leading or driving the llamas. Each drover is praying and asking the earth spirits for a safe trip.

The ceremony ends. The drovers and their helpers load the llamas with sacks of salt. The sacks are made of woven llama hair and are tied securely with ropes of braided llama hair. The salt was cut in blocks from salt flats near Lake Poopó. The llama drovers are traders who hope to exchange the salt for corn, herbs, and firewood from the valleys below.

The caravan heads out. The path from the village narrows between steep rocks. In some places the path is wide enough for only one llama at a time. This is dangerous because the llamas can scrape themselves badly on rocks. When the caravan stops, the drovers will inspect all the llamas and treat any with cuts.

The caravan keeps a steady pace. There will be no stopping until mid-afternoon. Then the drovers will choose a place with pasture and water. The llamas will be unloaded and allowed to graze. Helpers will build a fire and make a stew of potatoes and llama fat and bones.

This routine is repeated every day for two weeks. Finally the caravan reaches a valley dotted with small villages and fields. The caravan drovers stop at a village and look for the people they always deal with. Salt is exchanged for corn. The caravan goes from village to village, trading salt for more corn, until the salt is gone and the llamas are loaded with corn. Then the return trek to the mountains begins.

Llama caravans like this one were used far into the twentieth century. When Spaniards came to the Andes, they used llamas to transport metal from mines in the mountains to seaports. For the native Americans of the Andes the llama was an important link in a trading system that provided goods for both mountain and valley people.

1. Why did people who lived in the mountains need to trade goods?

2. Besides being a beast of burden, in what other ways was the llama useful to native Americans of the Andes?

3. The use of llama caravans declined when villagers began to buy trucks to carry goods. Describe two or three ways this transportation change might have changed life for people in the mountains and the valleys.

Building Vocabulary

Below are four groups of words. Use the words in each group in a brief paragraph that describes some aspect of American history you have read about in Part 4. Each group of words should be used in a separate paragraph.

1. Hopi
pueblo
kiva
sipapu

2. Iroquois
Council of
   Sachems
Iroquois League
democracy

3. Kwakiutl
potlatch
surplus
respect

4. Aztec
chocolate
tomato
avocado

PART
5

AFRICA

In East Africa, on the slopes of Mount Kilimanjaro (kihl-uh-muhn-JAHR-oh), a group of teenagers has just come out of their mountain school. The sun shines brightly. The young people look up to see the sunshine sparkle off the snow-covered peaks far above them.

One of the students is carrying a history textbook. The textbook was written by a British historian. Before 1960, Britain ruled this part of Africa.

The students are laughing at something they have just read in the textbook. The book says that Mount Kilimanjaro was "discovered" in 1847 by a German explorer. The students roared when they read this. They knew that their ancestors had lived on the mountain for many centuries before the Germans came! "How can they say that the mountain was discovered in 1847?" one student asks her teacher. "We were here when they arrived."

The Mystery of Africa. The truth is that Westerners knew very little about the interior of Africa until the nineteenth century. Until then, Africa was a "dark continent," a place of mystery. Some Westerners had read about Africa in books. But what they had read was often a mixture of fact and fantasy. One well-known book had a report from a group of Roman explorers who traveled south from Egypt about 77 A.D. The book described human beings with strange features—like monsters. Some African people, said the book, had no noses. Others had no tongues. And some had no nostrils for breathing. It is easy for us to laugh at such wild tales. In earlier times, however, many Westerners at least half-believed them.

Why did Westerners know so little about Africa? Because most of the continent was cut off from the outside world. Explorers who tried to learn about Africa faced many challenges. That was mainly because of Africa's geography.

For one thing, Africa's coastline is mostly straight. Sailors find few natural harbors where they feel safe in anchoring their ships. What's more, waterfalls and other hazards block all of Africa's main rivers. Boats can get only so far and no farther.

Africa does contain many possible land routes. Some have been used for centuries. For example, major trade routes run from western and central Africa to western Asia and the lands along the Mediterranean Sea. However, all of those routes cross the world's largest desert, the Sahara (suh-HAR-uh). Travel across the hot, dry Sahara is very difficult.

Leather, plant fiber, and wood mask worn in religious dances. Wood carving of antelopes. Page 144: Bronze plaque of Benin king (center) and two warriors.

For these and other reasons, Westerners remained ignorant of Africa for centuries. They made contact only with groups who lived along Africa's coasts. From those groups, Westerners bought slaves. They also engaged in limited trade in other goods, such as gold. Such contacts began during the fifteenth century. But few Westerners knew or cared much about Africa's long and complex past. As late as the 1930's, many history books barely mentioned the continent.

Today we know much more. We know that wealthy trading empires and complex governments existed in Africa as far back as the time of the Egyptian pharaohs (FEHR-ohz). We have found signs that the human race itself may have begun in Africa.

In this section, you will learn of the peoples who were part of Africa's early history. In Africa, as in the Americas, there were many different groups. Each had its own traditions and ways of living.

22
Traces from the Distant Past

For more than 30 years, Louis and Mary Leakey had been digging in the earth of Africa. The Leakeys were *anthropologists* (an-thruh-PAHL-uh-juhsts). That is, they were scientists who study human cultures, past and present. The Leakeys, for all those years, had been looking for the very first humans.

An Important Discovery. It was a hot July day in 1959. The Leakey's camp was in a deep gorge, or canyon. The gorge was located in eastern Africa. It was in what is now the nation of Tanzania (tan-zuh-NEE-uh).

The early morning sun baked the ground. The air felt like steam—hot and wet. Louis Leakey felt ill.

"You must stay in the tent and rest. Don't come out with me today," Mary said. She went out to continue their digging. She promised to be back before sundown.

Late in the day, as the sun began to drop behind the trees, Mary Leakey spotted something. It was buried in a slab of ancient rock. Carefully, she dug it out. It was a hunk of bone.

Eagerly, Mary Leakey examined her find. She saw that the ancient bone was part of a jaw. With it were some upper teeth. To her trained eyes, the jaw and teeth appeared to be human.

Mary Leakey ran to get her husband. She woke him and told him to come with her. She showed him what she had found.

Why was she so thrilled to find a few pieces of bone?

Scientists have long wondered about the beginnings of the human race. When did humans first appear? And where?

Early Discoveries. Early in this century, anthropologists searched for ancient human remains. In Asia they found

Olduvai (OHL-duh-vee) Gorge in Tanzania where the Leakeys discovered pieces of bone and implements possibly from the world's first humans.

bones from several humans who lived about half a million years ago. From those findings, many scientists believed that the human race had started in Asia. They thought the human race must be about half a million years old.

However, evidence found in south-eastern Africa suggested a different story. In 1925, two scientists found part of a skull buried deep in the earth. The skull appeared to be nearly two million years old. The skull was like a human skull in many ways. Did it come from a

human? Or did it come from an ape? How could they be sure?

One way scientists can tell human bones from nonhuman ones is by examining the items found with the bones. Early humans made and used tools such as sharpened rocks and sticks. Nonhumans did not. Scientists who found the skull in southeastern Africa had found either a human or an ape.

Then, in 1959, Louis and Mary Leakey made their find in eastern Africa. The ancient jaw and teeth that Mary Leakey had found belonged to a humanlike creature. From the age of the rocks, the Leakeys knew that the creature had lived about two million years ago.

With more digging, the Leakeys found 400 pieces of bone. They were able to put the pieces together to form almost a whole skull. Then the Leakeys made their most exciting discovery of all. Close to the ancient bones they found small stones with sharp edges. Someone had split and pounded the stones to sharpen them. That someone must have been human!

The Leakeys' discovery forced scientists to change their minds about when the human race began. Humans were much older than scientists had thought. They were probably at least two million years old. And Africa, not Asia, now seemed to be the birthplace of the human race.

The Search Continues. Since 1959, anthropologists have continued to explore the dawn of human life. They have found even older bones in Africa. In Ethiopia (ee-thee-OH-pee-uh), in 1974, a scientist found the bones of a female creature he called "Lucy." Lucy lived about three million years ago. She seems to have been more like an ape than like a human. But some scientists believe she was a direct ancestor of early humans.

Other scientists have tried a different approach. They work in a laboratory and not outdoors. They have looked for a sort of "clock" that would tick off the ages of human existence.

For example, some scientists have found new and better ways of measuring the ages of rocks. Now, when people like Mary Leakey find bones in rocks, it is easier to guess the age of the bones.

Other scientists have used microscopes and other tools to "look" deep inside the human body. They study tiny particles called molecules (MAHL-ih-kyools). Molecules are like "building blocks." They make up bones and other body parts. By studying molecules, scientists have tried to tell how closely humans are related to apes and other creatures. They think they know how recently apes and humans had a common ancestor. Their estimate: about five million years ago.

Scientists do not always agree on points like these. In fact, they often disagree. There are many different theories about how old the human race really is. So the search goes on for more bones, more early tools. How far back can scientists trace our family tree? No one can know for sure. It looks as if the search will go on for many years to come.

✎ Quick Check

1. *What is the work of anthropologists?*

2. *Why was the 1959 discovery of bones by Mary and Louis Leakey important?*

3. *How do scientists tell the difference between human and nonhuman bones?*

4. *According to the present understanding of scientists, when and where did the human race probably begin?*

5. *Why do scientists need a "clock" for telling the age of rocks and bones?*

150

23
The Spears That Won a Battle

For more than a thousand years, the most powerful people in Africa were the Egyptians. Although desert lands lay all around, Egypt had green fields and plenty of food. It prospered because it had water. The main source of water was the Nile River, which flowed north through Egypt to the Mediterranean Sea.

The Land of Kush. Before the Nile reached Egypt, it passed through a land called Kush. Kush lay south of Egypt, in what is now Sudan (soo-DAN). Like Egypt, Kush had green fields near the Nile. Some of its people were farmers. Others raised cattle. Kush was rich in natural resources such as gold and copper.

About 2600 B.C., Egypt sent soldiers to attack Kush. To get there, soldiers had to pass a series of waterfalls called *cataracts* (KAT-uh-rakts). The cataracts made travel to the south a challenge. But the Egyp-

tians overcame that challenge. They defeated Kush and captured many prisoners.

For almost 2,000 years, Kush remained a small and weak country. Much of that time it was under Egyptian rule. Traders went back and forth between Egypt and Kush. They carried gold, ebony, ivory, cattle, and slaves north to Egypt. Many Egyptians went to live in Kush. They built temples to Egyptian deities. The people of Kush learned to worship Egyptian gods and goddesses and to live much as the Egyptians lived.

Then Egypt weakened. This period of weakness began about 1100 B.C. Kush became independent, with its own king. As the Egyptians grew weaker, Kush grew stronger.

The royal family of Kush built a strong army. In 752 B.C., that army invaded Egypt. The Kushites won battle after bat-

tle. Before long, the little Kingdom of Kush had conquered all of Egypt.

For nearly 100 years, the kings of Kush ruled over both Egypt and Kush. But in 671 B.C., Assyrians (uh-SIHR-ee-uhns) from western Asia marched into Egypt. They challenged the Kushites in battle. Their iron weapons overpowered the Kushites. Let's imagine what an army general from Kush might have said about it all.

How could we know on that bright morning of battle how dark the night would be? The warm air chills me now. My eyes seek comfort in the dark grays of evening. My ears still ring from the cries of battle.

My job was to defend the mighty King of Kush and all his lands. But I failed. I had no idea that our enemies were so strong.

On the morning of battle, I looked at my army and was proud. The men stood firm and straight. I could see that their stone spears were sharp. We moved silently to the north.

At daybreak of the third day, we found the Assyrians. The sun was still low and red in the morning sky. They were waiting to do battle with us.

"For the honor of the King of Kush— forward!" I cried. I watched my son lead the first charge. I saw him raise his spear high over his head. I saw him gulp the air as he ran, and then—

A bolt of silver! How can I say it? A spear that shone as if it contained sun-

light! It struck my son, who screamed in surprise—and fell dead.

This was no ordinary spear. It was made not of stone but of metal. It was made of iron.

"Forward!" I cried again. My men ran forward. The horrible crash of stone against metal filled my ears.

"What weapons are these?" my second-in-command shouted. "How can we fight such an army with sticks and stones?"

I had no answer for him. Our men were falling. Many lay dead or wounded. Blood flowed across the ground.

I saw that the battle was lost. I called retreat. Our band of soldiers fled south, to safety.

Now my heart is heavy. My eyes swim in tears. How can I face my King again? What can I say that will ease the pain of our loss? When—if ever—will Kush again be a mighty power on the battlefield?

A Kingdom Built on Iron. The Kingdom of Kush never again ruled Egypt. But the Kushites had learned an important lesson from their defeat. They had seen the importance of iron.

Kush had natural resources to produce its own iron. Around the city of Meroe (MEHR-uh-wee) there was wood for fuel and there was iron ore. Meroe became Kush's capital. It became one of the biggest iron-making cities of the ancient world.

The people of Meroe made iron weap-

Kush temple with Greek-style columns and ornamentation

ons for Kush's soldiers. The soldiers used them to attack enemies to the south. Toolmakers also used iron. They fashioned iron hoes for farming. The hoes helped the farmers of Kush to grow more grain. From Meroe, the knowledge of ironworking spread to the south and west.

For hundreds of years, Kush remained an important kingdom. Its people continued to follow the Egyptian religion. Priests in Kush used the Egyptian style of writing with hieroglyphs. But they used different symbols than the Egyptians had. Today we cannot read what they wrote.

The rulers of Kush were powerful and proud. They had themselves buried in giant pyramids, like those of the Egyptians. The royal family included important queens. Romans who visited Kush in 77 A.D. said they found a queen ruling over Meroe. Her name was Candace.

After the first century A.D., Kush began to weaken. Desert tribes attacked from the west. In the east, a new country called Axum (AHK-soom) had appeared. It was centered in what is now Ethiopia. Soldiers of a Christian king of Axum defeated Kush about the year 350 A.D. After that, Kush vanished from the pages of history.

✎ Quick Check

1. *Why was Kush important to the Egyptians?*

2. *What ideas and practices did the Kushites borrow from the Egyptians?*

3. *Why were the Assyrians able to defeat the Kushites?*

4. *How did Meroe become one of the ancient world's chief centers of iron making?*

5. *What brought about the weakening of Kush?*

24
Kingdom of Gold

If you had traveled west from the ancient kingdom of Kush, you would have crossed an immense grassland. The grassland is called the Sudan. It reached all the way across Africa to the Atlantic Ocean. After traveling many weeks, you would have reached the Western Sudan. To the north lay a desert—the Sahara. To the south lay forests.

In the grassy plains of the Western Sudan, a new kingdom was taking shape about the time of Kush's fall. Its name was Ghana (GAHN-uh). The people who lived there were called the Soninke (soh-NIHN-keh).

Historians now believe that ancient Ghana began west of the Niger (NY-juhr) River bend between 300 and 500 A.D. By that time, knowledge of ironworking had spread across the Sudan. The early people of Ghana knew how to make iron tools and weapons. Some of their neigh-bors were slower to learn the new ways. That gave the people of Ghana an advantage.

Crossroads of Trade. The people of Ghana had another advantage—their location. They lived along an important trade route. Ghana became rich by handling two-way trade between people of the desert and people of the forest.

The people of the Sahara desert were called Berbers (BUHR-buhrz). They were traders who crossed the desert in large groups, or caravans. Each caravan had many camels carrying heavy loads. The caravans traveled at night to escape the burning sun.

Going south, the camels carried blocks of salt. All people need salt in their diet. People in hot places need even more salt because they lose salt when they sweat. Salt was mined in parts of the Sahara. The people of the desert had more salt

وَافْرِي أَدِيْمَ فَذْفِذِ فَفَذَ فِذٍ وَاقْتَنِعِي بِالنَّشْرِ عِنْدَا لْمَوْرِدِ

Arab merchants, like this one from a thirteenth-century drawing, carried salt across the desert to trade for Sudanese gold.

than they needed. The people of the forests were willing to pay a lot for salt. Sometimes they were so desperate that they bought salt for its weight in gold.

Going north, the camels carried lumps, or nuggets, of gold. Most of the precious metal came from forests in the south. The Berbers could buy many things with the gold. They traded some of it to seafaring people who took the gold to Europe. There it was made into coins and jewelry. Gold from the Ghana trade might grace the neck of a princess in Europe.

Ghana at this time was governed by a king. For four hundred years, the kings were Berbers from the north. Then, in about 770, the native Soninke rose up against the Berber kings and took control of the government.

The king of Ghana and his officials had many advantages. The king charged a tax on all goods passing through his kingdom. Although Ghana had little natural wealth, the king and his people grew rich by acting as go-betweens in the gold-salt trade.

At this time, centers of trade were growing into towns. Artisans in the towns made goods from ivory, leather, metal, and wood. Traders bought those goods too. They took them north across the desert. When they returned, they brought other items along with salt. They brought swords, copper pots, and silks.

DESERT TRAFFIC

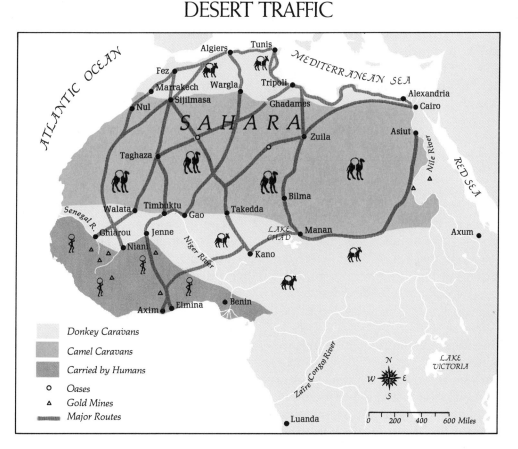

The map shows how goods were moved along the ancient African trade routes. Use the map to answer the following questions:

1. Locate Africa on the world map, page 214. What part of Africa is shown on this map?

2. What means of transport would move a merchant's goods from Fez to Timbuktu?

3. How was gold transported from the mines to Timbuktu?

Another item of trade was slaves. Sometimes the Berbers and Soninke bought slaves. More often they sold them. Ghana had fierce soldiers. They would attack small villages and capture many people to be sold as slaves.

After a time, Muslim Arabs as well as Berbers crossed the desert to trade. The Arabs came from western Asia. They conquered northwestern Africa about 670. There, they spread the religion of Islam to the people. Many Berbers became Muslims.

The Arabs were impressed with the wealthy country they found. Some Arab visitors described Ghana's royal court about 1065. The king was thought to be like a god. To show respect, his subjects fell on their knees before him. They threw dust on their heads. The king wore a cap trimmed with gold. Necklaces glittered from his neck, and bracelets from his wrists. Even the dogs that guarded the king had collars of gold and silver.

The king's lands covered a large part of the Western Sudan and nearby forests. The kingdom included many states or provinces. Each had its own ruler who served under the king of Ghana.

Ghana was then at the height of its power. About this time Ghana's capital was a city called Koumbi (KOOM-bee). Koumbi was perhaps the biggest city in West Africa. It had about 15,000 people.

Invasion. But Koumbi met the fate of many capitals. It was conquered and destroyed. The conquerors were Muslim Berbers known as Almoravids (al-moh-RAH-vihdz). The Almoravids built a great empire in northwest Africa and southern Spain. They sent soldiers into the Western Sudan. Ghana's soldiers fought the Almoravids for more than 20 years. Finally, in 1076, the Almoravids conquered Koumbi and destroyed it.

The Almoravids tried to rule Ghana themselves. But revolts broke out in many places. Most of the non-Muslim people of Ghana were unhappy with Muslim rule. They resented Almoravid efforts to convert them to Islam.

The Almoravids lost control in about 1087. For another century or so, the kingdom of Ghana lived on. But without a central government, it was only a shadow of its old self. Many great cities lost their trade and shrunk to villages.

The glory of ancient Ghana is remembered even today. The name Ghana is still in use. It was taken in 1957 by a new country that lies south and east of ancient Ghana. Some of the people of today's Ghana claim to be descendants of the earliest Ghana people.

✎ Quick Check

1. *How did Ghana's location help it to become a great kingdom?*

2. *Who were the Berbers? Why were they important in Ghana?*

3. *How did the king of Ghana and his officials grow rich?*

4. *Why were Arab traders impressed by Ghana?*

5. *What was the capital of Ghana? Why did it decline?*

25
The Hungering Lion

The kingdom of Ghana had crumbled. What remained were many small states, each under its own ruler. The states fought one another for control of the gold and salt trade.

A showdown between two peoples would soon lead to a new and powerful kingdom. The kingdom of Mali (MAHL-ee) would grow even bigger and richer than Ghana. But first its people, the Mandingos (man-DING-gohz), had to defeat their powerful enemies, the Sossos (SO-soz). How this happened is an interesting story. It should be told by a Mandingo storyteller.

Children and adults sat together on the ground. The small village in the kingdom of Mali was very still. All that could be heard was the barking of a dog in the distance. The storyteller began the story of how Mali came to be:

The Mandingo people and the Sossos spoke the same language and had the same ancestors. But they were enemies. The Sossos were led by the cruel king Sumanguru (soo-man-GOO-roo). Sumanguru was hated by all the Mandingos. When the Mandingo king died, Sumanguru took control of our land. He made us pay high taxes to him. He took our food and our gold.

The old king of the Mandigos had left 12 sons. Sumanguru did not want any of them to challenge him. He took 11 of the boys and had them put to death. The twelfth boy was named Sundiata (soon-dee-AH-ta). That means "hungering lion."

Sundiata was just a child. But it was easy to see that he wasn't much of a lion. He was small and weak. Part of his body was paralyzed. He couldn't even stand up. No one thought he would ever walk. His mother took him to healers in all parts of the kingdom. But none of them had any hope for him.

Sumanguru took one look at the boy and laughed. "This one can live!" Sumanguru cried. "He will never be any threat to me. I will rule over the Mandingo people forever."

Sumanguru had made a big mistake. Sundiata was weak in body—but strong in spirit. He refused to give in to the sickness that kept him from standing. He forced himself to stand on both legs. He worked until he dropped.

After months and months of painful exercise, he won another victory: He got himself to walk. He had to use a cane—but he was walking.

He kept working to build up his body. Soon he could throw away the cane. Before long, he could walk without even a limp. Then he taught himself to ride a horse. He learned to hunt and to use weapons.

"Now at last I am ready," Sundiata told his friends. "Now I will lead my people against Sumanguru and the Sossos."

And that is what happened. Sundiata was made king of the Mandingos. The people were proud of their brave young king. But they warned him about Sumanguru. "He knows how to use witchcraft," they told Sundiata. "How will we fight against magic powers?"

"With powers of our own," Sundiata said. "Just as I rose up against my illness, we shall rise up against Sumanguru and his witchcraft!"

This promise led to a famous battle. The two mighty armies met near a village called Karina (kah-REE-nah). Sumanguru used all the magic he knew. But Sundiata's magic was better. His army was winning the battle.

At last Sundiata raised his bow and took aim at Sumanguru. He hit him with an arrow tipped with the spur of a white rooster. Sumanguru disappeared into the skies. On the spot where he stood, a large tree sprang up.

And that is the story of Sundiata, the Hungering Lion. And this is how we won our fight against the Sossos and how the mighty kingdom of Mali began. Now the moon is high. My story is over for tonight.

Obviously, the storyteller's tale is not completely true. What parts of the story just could not have happened? What parts could be true? Stories such as this one have a great importance in understanding ancient history. Why should that be so? It is because such stories were passed from one generation to another among people who did not write down their history. Without such stories, parts of a people's history might be lost.

The battle between Sumanguru and Sundiata took place in 1235. Mali became the mightiest kingdom of the Western Sudan. Its king, or *mansa* (MAHN-suh), and some of its people became Muslims. One king, Mansa Musa (MAHN-suh MOO-suh), gained fame for his great wealth. On a trip through Egypt in 1324, he took 100 camel loads of gold. Few Egyptians had ever seen such riches.

In time, however, Mali's power declined. When a king died, quarrels broke out over who should be the new king. Enemies attacked from many sides. Mali lost its outer provinces. By the 1500's Mali was a small and unimportant state.

161

Eight miles from the Niger River, on the edge of the Sahara Desert, Timbuktu was an important trade center.

Rise of Songhay. Another people, the Songhays (SONG-gayz), built a strong new Muslim kingdom east of Mali. The kingdom was called Songhay, after its people. For a time, Songhay had been ruled by Mali. Then it had thrown off Mali's rule. Songhay began to expand in the 1460's. Songhay took control of the gold-salt trade. Its kings built the richest and best organized state the Western Sudan had yet seen. Songhay ruled an area larger than Western Europe.

Some of Songhay's cities won fame as centers of Muslim learning. The most famous city was Timbuktu (tihm-buhk-TOO). Timbuktu had once been part of Mali. Then Songhay took it over. A visitor from North Africa about 1520 was very impressed. He wrote: "More profit is made from selling books in Timbuktu

162

than from any other branch of trade."

But Songhay did not last. In 1591 an army from Morocco, in northwest Africa, crossed the Sahara. It attacked Songhay. The attacking army was smaller than Songhay's army. But the attackers had guns. Songhay's soldiers had only spears and arrows. The attackers won. Songhay—like Ghana and Mali before it—faded into history.

✎ Quick Check

1. Why were the Mandingos and the Sossos enemies?

2. Why did Sumanguru let Sundiata live?

3. Why are tales told by storytellers important to a people's history?

4. How did Songhay become great?

5. Why were visitors impressed by the city of Timbuktu?

KINGDOMS OF THE SUDAN

Kingdom of Ghana
11th Century A.D.

Kingdom of Mali
14th Century A.D.

Kingdom of Songhay
16th Century A.D.

The Senegal and the Niger rivers were the sites of three great kingdoms. Use the maps to answer the following questions:

1. Locate Africa on the world map, page 214. What part of Africa is shown on these maps?

2. The three maps tell a long story about the Western Sudan. How many centuries of history do the maps show?

3. In 1076 the Almoravids conquered and destroyed Koumbi. This brought to an end one of the kingdoms. Which one?

26
Spreading Out

Up to now we have looked at the part of Africa lying directly south of the Sahara. But what about the central and southern parts of the continent? Those parts, too, have a rich and varied history.

Bantu Peoples. Historians believe that central and southern Africa were very lightly settled until about 2,000 years ago. Then new people began to move in. The new people came from West Africa. They moved in separate groups at different times. But they all spoke varieties of an ancient language known as Bantu (BAN-too). For that reason, we call these people the Bantus.

You have already read about some Bantu peoples. The Soninke people of Ghana and the Mandingo people of Mali were called Bantus because of the languages they spoke.

Even before the time of Ghana and Mali, some groups of Bantus were on the move. They carried their knowledge of iron making into many parts of Africa. The Bantus had first lived in grasslands, but as they moved they came to great forests. They farmed and hunted with the aid of iron tools. With plenty of food, their group increased in number.

Hundreds of years passed. The Bantus spread over almost all of central and southern Africa. In some places the Bantus met other peoples. In time, some of these other peoples began to use Bantu words and married into Bantu families.

Rich Deposits of Gold. Some of the Bantus settled in southeastern Africa. They moved into the area between the Zambezi (zam-BEE-zee) and Limpopo (lim-POH-poh) Rivers. The high ground between those rivers held rich deposits of gold. Someone walking across a hill might have seen a flash of gold in the rocky ground. It would not have been hard to chip a soft piece of gold from the ground. But getting larger amounts of gold was another matter. That was hard work. People had to hammer iron points into the rock. They had to dig out the vein of gold, which might go deep into the ground.

By about 400 A.D., African peoples had begun to mine the Zambezi-Limpopo gold. They dug deep holes straight down, following the veins of gold. Many of the miners were girls and women. Their bodies were small enough to slip down a narrow shaft and dig the gold at the bottom.

The work could be very dangerous. Many women fell to their deaths. Others were crushed when the walls of a shaft caved in. Searchers have found the bones of people who were killed in those early mines. That is how we know that many of the miners were women.

By 1100, if not earlier, the Zambezi-Limpopo gold had become part of a thriving trade. Africans carried the gold to the Indian Ocean. There they met Arab traders who came by boat. In exchange for gold, the Arabs gave cloth, glass beads, and other goods. Some of the goods came from as far away as India and China.

Builders of Zimbabwe. One group of people in the Zambezi-Limpopo area began to put up large buildings about 1100.

They built thick stone walls that rose high in the air. Ancient stone buildings have been found in many places between the Zambezi and the Limpopo. But the biggest and most famous buildings are at a place called Zimbabwe (zihm-BAHB-wee). Zimbabwe means "stone houses."

Zimbabwe was the capital of an important kingdom. It was governed by the Shona (SHOH-nuh) people, a branch of the Bantus. They began to build Zimbabwe about 1100.

If you visited Zimbabwe today, you would find many of the stone walls in ruins. But the walls are still awesome. Some of them rise as high as a three-story building. At their base, they are as wide as three automobiles parked side by side.

At first, the builders of Zimbabwe did not think about making their buildings pretty. They only wanted them to be sturdy. Eventually, more skillful builders worked on the buildings. They laid the stones in special patterns.

In the hands of the new builders, the walls grew even sturdier and taller. There was no mortar to hold the stones together. There were no square corners. But the stones fit together almost perfectly.

The walls at Zimbabwe served many purposes. Some were for homes. They were covered with roofs of sticks and leaves. Others enclosed raised terraces where crops were grown. Some of the biggest walls seem to have been part of temples, where religious ceremonies took place.

166

One large structure was probably the king's palace. The people of Zimbabwe considered their king a deity. They crawled on the ground when he was present. Most of them were not even allowed to look at him. A few favored ones were, and they flattered him by imitating his every move.

Wealth from Trade. Zimbabwe was wealthy from its trade in gold and ivory. People could measure their wealth in small copper bars, which were used for money. To protect their wealth and land, they had a strong army. This was very important in dry years. Many farmers and herdspeople lived to the east of Zimbabwe, on the edge of a great desert called the Kalahari (kahl-uh-HAHR-ee). When there was little rain, they would try to move to the richer lands of Zimbabwe. But the army was usually there to keep them out.

Zimbabwe is no longer the capital of a great kingdom. Its buildings were destroyed by enemies. The last king was killed in 1834. But the fame of ancient Zimbabwe lives on. The name now is used by a nation that is almost as large as California. The country includes the Zimbabwe ruins. It took the name Zimbabwe when it became independent from Britain in 1980.

✎ Quick Check

1. *Who are the Bantus? When did they move into central and southern Africa?*

2. *What happened to the African peoples who already lived in those areas?*

3. *Which peoples founded Zimbabwe? How did Zimbabwe grow wealthy?*

4. *How were the walls of Zimbabwe used? Why did they last a long time?*

5. *Why did Zimbabwe have a strong army?*

Without mortar, these 800-foot granite walls at Zimbabwe (near modern Nyanda) still stand 32 feet high.

27
Tradition and Change

Little by little, the migrating Bantu peoples finally settled in new villages. As they did, they began to build their own ways of life. In the forests, most people hunted for their food or planted root crops. In the grasslands, some kept cattle and others grew grain. Some did both.

Nearly all of these people shared certain basic ideas. They placed great importance on family ties. They thought that everyone should marry and raise children. They believed that a god or gods watched over their lives. But most of these people lived in small groups. As a result, many of their traditions differed from village to village.

Here are glimpses of life in three Bantu villages before 1850. What do these stories tell you about the things many Africans had in common?

The night is warm and pleasant. Nzinga (un-ZING-guh) creeps closer to the fire. If the men see him, they may tell him to go away. He is only 11. But if he keeps quiet, they will pretend not to see him.

Nzinga is a member of the royal family of Kongo (KAHN-goh). His village lies south of the Zaire (zah-EER) River, in central Africa. It is in an area that will one day be part of Angola.

Nzinga's father, Affonso (ah-FOHN-soh), is speaking. When Affonso was born, he too had been called Nzinga. Then—in the 1480's—white men from Europe came to Kongo. They persuaded the royal family and many others to become Christians. Members of the family took new, Christian names. Nzinga's father took a name that had been used by

Benin ivory carving of Portuguese with sword, spear, and cross

kings in Portugal, the country from which the white men came.

It is easy to see that Affonso is angry. He is speaking in a loud voice. The men around the fire respond by nodding and adding their own angry statements. They are important men, advisers to the King.

"It is a disgrace," says Affonso. "The white merchants pay no attention to our laws. They send men deep into our country to get slaves. They go to our village leaders. They ask the leaders to capture the people of other villages and sell them as slaves. Sometimes the white men even make war on our villages. They capture slaves themselves."

"You are right. Matters are out of hand," says the oldest adviser. "My own brother's sons have been carried away to be slaves."

If this keeps up, our villages will be empty. Our people will all be gone," says Affonso.

"The village leaders are weak men," says a second adviser. "They want the goods that the merchants bring. They are willing to make war to get slaves for trading."

"But what can we do?" asks the first adviser.

"We can protest to the king of Portugal," replies Affonso. "I will send the king a message. I will tell him that this slave-taking must stop. Surely the white men's king will listen to me, a fellow king."

Nzinga has moved too close. One of the men suddenly turns around. "Go away!" says the man.

Brooding over what he has heard, Nzinga walks back to his mother's hut. He shudders to think of the men who catch and sell slaves. "What if they should come after me?" he thinks. With relief, Nzinga sees the glow of his mother's fire. For now, at least, he is safe.

One thousand five hundred miles to the southeast, Manyami (man-YAH-mee) is walking back to his village. Manyami belongs to the Ndebele (un-duh-BEH-leh) people. His village is in southern Africa, not far from ancient Zimbabwe.

Three days ago Manyami bathed in a nearby stream. Then he walked out to stay among the trees and tall grasses. He could not eat anything in the daytime. The other boys of the village kept an eye on him. Manyami believed that the great god Unkulunkulu (oon-koo-LOON-koo-loo) was watching too.

Manyami walks back into the circle of round huts. He goes up to the village doctor. The doctor mixes flour with special herbs. He dips one end of a stick into the mixture. Then he points the stick at Manyami.

Manyami grips the stick in his mouth and swallows some of the mixture. Then the doctor takes the stick and hits Manyami three times. Manyami does not move or make a sound.

In Manyami's part of Africa, most boys go through some kind of ceremony when they are about 14. The Ndebele ceremony is one of the simplest. By leaving his home for three days, a young person "breaks away" from his childhood. By taking the blows from the stick, he shows that he is tough.

Now it's official. Manyami is a man. And now he can look forward to another ritual—marriage.

One thousand five hundred miles to the north, a Kikuyu (kih-KOO-yoo) couple has been married. Before the wedding, the groom's parents made a gift of

The Ndebele, a Bantu people, paint the walls of their huts and villages with a variety of geometric patterns.

An elder and law enforcement officer of the Kikuyu tribe 60 miles from Nairobi.

animals to the bride's parents. They gave one cow, 10 sheep, and 10 goats.

The Kikuyu live in East Africa, in what is now the nation of Kenya (KEEN-yuh). This is right on the Equator. Much of the land is so high that the weather never gets too hot. There are rolling hills and many small farms. There are also grasslands where cattle, sheep, and goats can graze.

This morning, the women in the groom's family went to fetch the bride. They carried her back on their shoulders. Like all Kikuyu brides, she pretended to struggle. She kept calling out, "I don't want to get married!"

Now it is evening, and she is celebrating with her friends. Young people of her own age are sitting with her outside the hut. The bride and the girls are singing special songs called "weeping." Once again, the bride is supposed to be sorry that she is giving up her single life.

But she is glad. She hopes to have at least four children—two boys and two girls. Those four will stand for her own parents and her husband's parents. They will keep the stream of life flowing from age to age.

The family is important for the Kikuyu. They believe that only God can live without parents or children.

Europeans Come to Africa. The Portuguese were the first of many Europeans to reach sub-Saharan Africa (Africa south of the Sahara). The Dutch and the English soon followed. Around 1700, Dutch settlers started moving inland from the southern tip of Africa. They fought wars against Bantu peoples like the Zulus (ZOO-looz). Dutch and English settlers founded what is now the country of South Africa.

During the 1800's, other Europeans moved into Africa. They took control of much of the continent. They set up colonies and ruled over African peoples. The Africans tried to win back their freedom. But many years passed before they succeeded. Since the 1950's most African colonies have gained their freedom. Sub-Saharan Africa now has more than 35 independent countries.

*Voortrekkers making the Great Trek from the Cape Colony
to Natal between 1835 and 1843.*

Africa's history has produced a rich—and sometimes explosive—mixture of peoples and customs. Perhaps the most explosive mixture today is in the country of South Africa. There are nearly 5 million white people in South Africa. There are also 26 million blacks, Asians, and people of mixed races. Whites run the government but blacks and others have demanded more rights. The struggle for control of South Africa has produced great suffering in recent years.

✎ Quick Check

1. *How did Portuguese merchants get slaves from Kongo?*

2. *What did Manyami have to do before he could be considered a man?*

3. *How did Kikuyu marriage customs show that Kikuyus believed the family to be very important?*

4. *What European peoples settled the southern tip of Africa? When?*

5. *When did Africans in sub-Saharan Africa begin to win their freedom?*

BANTU LANDS

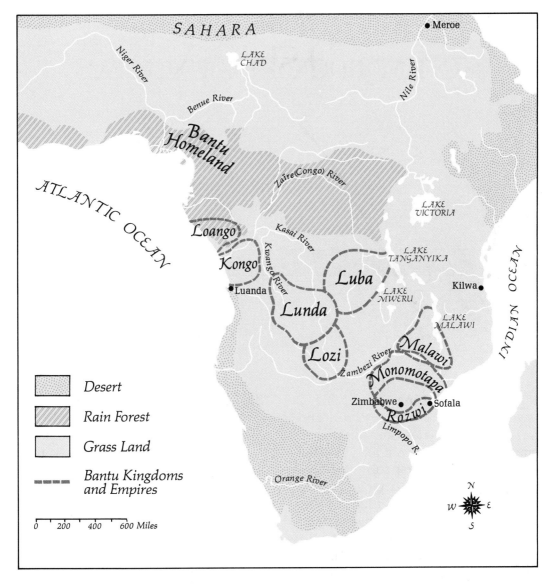

For hundreds of years the Bantu peoples migrated into central and southern Africa. Use the map to answer the following questions:

1. True or false? Most Bantu settlements were located in the rain forest region.

2. In which direction did the Bantu travel when they migrated from their homeland?

3. About how far was Zimbabwe from the Bantu homeland?

PART 5
Review and Skills Exercises

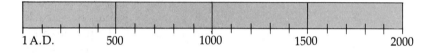

1 A.D.   500   1000   1500   2000

Designing a Time Line

As you read in Part 5, empires rose and fell in Africa. Time lines can show when an empire rose and when it fell. To make your own time line, first copy the time line grid above. Make it large enough to add information. Below is a list of West African empires and the dates of their duration. Add the information in the list to your time line. Then use your imagination. How can you show that empires lasted over a period of time? If your time line does not show this, try again.

300-1250	Empire of Ghana
650-1590	Empire of Songhay
1200-1500	Empire of Mali

Building Vocabulary Using Place Names

Write the numbers 1-5 on a sheet of paper to correspond to the seven sentences below. By each number write the word from the list that best completes each sentence.

1. The Kush lived south of Egypt in _____ .

2. The Soninke of _____ were ruled by Berber kings until 770.

3. According to legend, the Kingdom of _____ grew after its young king Sundiata, slew their enemy with a magic arrow.

4. _____ was a center of Muslim learning and the most famous city in the Songhay empire.

5. The Shona people built the great walls of _____ .

Kenya	Mali
Zimbabwe	Sudan
Ghana	Timbuktu

Interpreting a Legend

On pages 12 and 13 are photographs of art from the kingdom of Benin. This kingdom existed for hundreds of years in West Africa. Here is a legend from Benin that has come down through the centuries by word of mouth. Keep the following ideas in mind as you read the legend: People believed that before a person is born he or she kneels before the Creator and says what he or she wants to be in life. They believed that each person has a spiritual guide who stays behind in the land of the spirits. The guide's job is to help the person stay on their chosen path.

The Poor Man

Long ago there was a very poor man. Year after year this poor man planted crops. Year after year he had nothing to harvest, not a single yam. He asked the Creator, "Have I done evil deeds to deserve this poverty?"

At last his crops grew. At harvest time he took a basket to the field to pick his crops. What a sight he saw! Bush pigs had eaten every stem. The poor man followed the tracks of the bush pigs to the river. He jumped into the river and found himself at the palace of the Creator.

He told his sad tale to the Creator. The Creator locked him in a dark room and told him not to say a word. The man's spiritual guide came to see the Creator. The Creator said, "A poor man has been to see me. He has told me how much he has suffered."

The poor man's spiritual guide replied, "Yes, he is suffering. Let him suffer. When he went into the world he didn't say he wanted to be a farmer. He said he would be a trapper." The spiritual guide left.

The Creator unlocked the door and let out the poor man. "Did you hear your guide?" he asked. "Go back to the world and do what you said you would."

The poor man went back and began to set traps. As he pounded in a stick to hold a trap, he hit something hard. It was a pot full of beads of the most precious kind. The poor man sold the beads and became very rich.

From that day people have always said, "If you do not do what your spiritual guide has told you, you cannot prosper."

Answer the following questions on a separate piece of paper.

1. What kind of work did the man in the legend do and why was he poor?

2. Why was the man's spiritual guide not sympathetic to the man's sufferings?

3. Which of the following statements best sums up the moral, or advice, of this legend? Write the letter of your choice.

a. If a poor man can't grow crops, he should try trapping.

b. A person should do what he or she is cut out for in order to succeed.

c. If you are born poor, you will soon be rich.

PART
6

BYZANTINE AND MUSLIM EMPIRES

The following chapters concern two great Middle Eastern empires. Both lasted for hundreds of years. Both of them had rulers who conquered many distant lands. The first was the Byzantine (BIZ-un-teen) empire, centered in what is now Turkey. The second was the Muslim empire, which began on the Arabian Peninsula.

These two empires existed at about the same time. They were rivals for control of the Middle East. Of the two, the Byzantine empire was the older. This empire had its roots in both East and West. It began as the eastern half of the old Roman empire. From the beginning, however, it was as much a part of the Middle East as of Europe. The people in the empire called themselves Romans, even though the Western Roman empire was gone. Today we call them Byzantines.

The Byzantines had much in common with the Muslims. There were many similarities in their way of life. Western European travelers to the Middle East were shocked to see so little difference between the two groups. But the Byzantines differed from the Muslims in one important way. The Byzantines were Christians. The Muslims followed the faith of Islam. Both groups were very religious and were determined to protect their faiths and to spread them.

City at the Crossroads. At a crossroads between Europe and Asia stands a beautiful old city. Today we call it Istanbul (is-tan-BOOL). But for more than a thousand years that city was called Constantinople (kon-stan-tih-NOH-pul). It was the capital of the Byzantine empire.

The story of Constantinople and the Byzantine empire began with the Roman emperor Constantine (KON-stan-teen). He chose an old Greek town called Byzantium (buh-ZAN-she-uhm) for his capital. He picked the town for its location between the Mediterranean Sea and the Black Sea (see map on page 192). The town had hills where lookouts could spot ships or armies from far away. There was water on three sides, which made the town easy to defend.

Byzantium was also a crossroads of trade. The town controlled the waterways from Eastern to Western Europe. It also controlled some land routes used by merchants. People who wanted to take goods from Persia to Rome, for example, often passed through Byzantium.

Constantine had great plans for Byzantium when he moved his capital there in 330 A.D. He ordered miles of thicker, wider walls to be built along the city's

Trumpets announce the end of the Islamic month of fasting. Page 176: Ivory carving of St. Demetrius.

coasts. He also ordered Christian churches to be built. Constantine believed in the teachings of Jesus Christ. His city was the first Christian capital.

Constantine renamed the town "The New Rome That Is Constantine's City." That was a lot to say. So people called it Constantinople. From its old name, Byzantium, came the name Byzantine for the new empire.

Contributions of the Byzantine Empire. The rulers who followed Constantine built a government that lasted hundreds of years. The emperor (or at times the empress) held most of the power. The ruler claimed to speak for God. Christianity was the official religion.

As the years passed, the Byzantines came to seem strange to Western Europeans. Byzantine men and women took a lot of baths. They spoke Greek and knew how to read. They appreciated art, music, and theater. Even their table manners were different! One Byzantine princess married an Italian ruler. She had to teach her new subjects how to eat with forks.

To the educated people of the Byzantine world, Western Europeans seemed loud, dumb, and dirty. Few of them could read. Their clothes looked very plain next to the jewels and silks of Byzantine nobles. In addition, few Western Europeans ever saw Constantinople. It was too far away. So the two worlds drifted apart.

Byzantines came to feel more at home with people from Persia or India. In time, even the Byzantine Christian church split away from Western Europe. Byzantine church leaders no longer wanted the Roman Catholic pope in Rome to have any control over church affairs. In 1054 the Byzantine church declared its center to be in Constantinople, not Rome. It became the Eastern Orthodox Church.

In some ways, the cultural split helped Europe in later times. Why should that be so?

First, the Byzantines helped to save the learning of Greece and Rome. They saved the ideas and plays and poems of the ancient Western world. For hundreds of years, Europe was controlled by people who could not read. Western monks were able to save some books, but many more were lost. In the Byzantine world, however, old writings were preserved. We might not know about ancient Greek thinkers today if the Byzantines had not helped to keep their ideas alive.

Second, the Byzantines saved Roman laws. That was important because the Romans had been masters at making laws. Under their laws, people had known what was expected of them. They had also known their rights. Roman laws had given the Romans a strong sense of order. The Byzantines kept those laws and added to them. They made many of them more just and fair than laws had ever been in history.

Third, the Byzantines spread Christianity into Eastern Europe, including Russia. They did so through the work of missionaries. Missionaries also helped spread learning and writing. Christian missionaries went out from Constantinople beginning in the ninth century.

That is why many people of Yugoslavia, Bulgaria, and the Soviet Union are Orthodox Christians today.

Conflict in the Middle East. The Byzantine empire lasted longer than almost any empire in history. But it had many problems. One was that its leadership was very unstable. Emperors and empresses could not automatically pass the crown to their children. They had to name the future ruler while they were alive. Sometimes this was done by decree. Sometimes it was done by popular choice. This made it easy for other families to seize control of the empire. Nobles and generals plotted against their rulers in order to wear the crown. Most Byzantine rulers lost their crowns in some violent manner. Some were blinded. Others were murdered.

Another problem was the almost constant threat of attack from Muslim peoples. From the seventh century onward, Muslims were a powerful force in both the East and the West. They wanted to take over Byzantine lands, especially wealthy Constantinople.

Who would win in this struggle for land and power? Let's look at the two empires and find out.

St. Demetrius (left) one of the most popular saints of Orthodox Christianity, kills the Roman emperor, Diocletian, who persecuted Christians.

28
Justinian and Theodora

One of the greatest Byzantine emperors was Justinian (juh-STIN-ee-uhn). He was the son of a peasant who became a great general in the Byzantine army. When he took the throne in 527, Rome itself had fallen. Justinian set out to win back the Western European lands of the Roman empire. He believed that the whole world should be united under one emperor. Justinian and his armies were successful. They managed to recapture much of the territory of the old Roman empire (see map page 192).

But Justinian was far more than a fighter. He knew that a key strength of the Romans was the way they had run their government. He ordered a group of men to study all the old Roman laws. The men brought the old laws up to date. When two laws clashed, they chose one or the other. They wrote new laws, too. The result was a new set, or code, of laws. Today we call it the Justinian Code. Through that code, Roman law was passed on to the modern world.

Justinian changed his city as much as its laws. He had much of Constantinople rebuilt. When he was finished, people called it the Queen of Cities. Crowning the "queen" was an impressive church. It went by the Greek name Hagia Sophia (HAY-jee-ah soh-FEE-ah), meaning "Holy Wisdom." It glowed with gold, jewels, and a special Byzantine art called *mosaic* (moh-ZAY-ihk). Byzantine mosaics were pictures made of very tiny pieces of colored glass. Many mosaics told stories from the Bible.

Justinian's reign lasted from 527 to 565. But it might have ended sooner had it not been for his wife, Theodora (THEE-ah-dawr-ah). Theodora was a strong-minded, clever woman. Like Justinian, she was not born into a noble family.

Portion of a famous mosaic from a church in Ravenna, Italy. Emperor Justinian, standing between officials and clergymen, joins the church and state.

In this mosaic, also from Ravenna, Empress Theodora appears with officials and ladies-in-waiting.

Rather, it is said that her father kept bears for a circus in the Hippodrome, the capital's chief stadium. As a teenager, Theodora became an actress and a dancer. She was beautiful and admired by many. But the nobles looked down on her. Later, Theodora became interested in the Christian religion. She stopped performing. Then she met and married Justinian, who was about to inherit the throne.

When Justinian was crowned emperor, Theodora was crowned empress. The Byzantines were unusual for their time be-cause they allowed women to rule, either with their husbands or alone. Theodora helped set this trend. She shared in ruling the empire. Her steely nerves helped to give Justinian the confidence he needed to be a successful emperor.

Although Justinian and Theodora were successful rulers, their subjects sometimes grew restless. Five years into their rule, the city exploded in the Nika (NEE-kuh) Rebellion. Nika is a Greek battle cry that means "conquer." Many residents of Constantinople wanted to conquer the emperor and elect a new one.

The time: January, 532.

The place: the Hippodrome, Constantinople.

The scene: there is a pause between chariot races. They are a free entertainment for all the people of the city. Three spectators are talking.

BASIL: The whole city is complaining.

ALEX: It's no wonder. Justinian has raised taxes so high that all of us find it hard to make ends meet. First we had to pay for the war against the Persians in the East. Next we'll have to pay to fight the Vandals in the West. People say Justinian wants to restore our Roman empire to its old glory.

LEO: He has many grand ideas. Look at how he has tried to punish people who refuse to become Christians. And how he has tried to settle arguments among Christians themselves. He takes his religion very seriously!

ALEX: So does the empress. People say she has taken sides on questions of belief. She has tried to get the emperor to help the monks who are her friends. Many people think she is a meddler.

BASIL: Like you, I am unhappy with Justinian's high taxes. But you have to remember the good things that he and Theodora have done. Look at the beautiful buildings they have built. Look at the new hospitals for the poor.

LEO: If things don't change soon, we'll all be poor! I hear rumors of a plot to get rid of Justinian and Theodora. There is talk of crowning a new emperor.

ALEX: I would welcome such a deed.

BASIL: If we do get a new ruler, I hope it can be done peacefully.

The time: several days later.

The place: the Sacred Imperial Palace, by the sea.

The scene: mobs have set fire to parts of Constantinople. Many important buildings are destroyed. The emperor is talking to Leontius (lee-ON-tee-us), an aide. Theodora and a leading general look on.

JUSTINIAN: The people have gone mad. Have we any hope of restoring order?

LEONTIUS: There is no hope, your Majesty. The city is burning. The mob is trying to crown a new emperor. You must escape.

JUSTINIAN: Have we no soldiers to crush the mob?

LEONTIUS: Too many are away fighting in our wars. We have ordered ships to take you and her Majesty away.

JUSTINIAN: It makes me sick at heart. But if there is no choice, I will go. Theodora, we must hurry.

THEODORA: I must speak my mind. I hear your words with great sadness. I, for one, have a sense of dignity. I have worn the crown. Even if my life is in danger, I will not flee. If you want to go, Justinian, go. There is the sea. There are the steps to the sea. Go! For my part, I like the old saying "The empire is a fine burial cloth." I'll die an empress, not a coward.

JUSTINIAN: You give me courage.

THEODORA: It takes courage to stand and fight.

LEONTIUS: But, your Majesty—

JUSTINIAN: Silence! Theodora is right. General, am I to understand that the mobs are meeting now in the stadium?

GENERAL: Yes, your Majesty.

JUSTINIAN: How many people are assembled there?

GENERAL: Tens of thousands.

JUSTINIAN: So many? Hmmm. We can trap them. They will not be able to get out.

LEONTIUS: But what good will that do?

JUSTINIAN: The troops that I have left can crush the rebellion. It will prove to all my subjects that I mean to continue ruling the empire.

Justinian managed to put down the revolt in the Hippodrome. Almost 30,000 rebels were killed by his soldiers. Many officials who had participated in the revolt were stripped of their power.

A Strict but Fair Ruler. Although Justinian was ruthless when it came to protecting his throne, he usually had his subjects' best interests in mind. He believed that heavy taxes would be good for his people in the end. And his code of laws was designed to protect the human rights of his subjects. Rich people were not supposed to have more rights and privileges than poor people.

Many of the laws were strict but fair. In one famous case, Justinian punished a member of his own family who, he felt, had behaved unjustly. A poor woman had seen Justinian riding through the street and had thrown herself at his feet in tears. When questioned, she told him that the empress's brother was building a huge new palace next door to her house. The palace shadowed her house and made it dark and airless. When Justinian heard this, he ordered his brother-in-law to be beaten in public. The new palace was torn down and the property given to the woman.

Other laws in the code were even stricter. Justinian wanted to protect Christian beliefs from *heretics* (HEHR-eh-tihks)—people who disagreed with official church beliefs. And he wanted to punish people who he believed acted immorally. Heretics could not hold public office. Rapists and murderers could lose an eye or a hand or could be put to death.

Many years after Justinian's death in 565, his code of laws became a model for lawmakers in Western Europe. Justinian's Code still influences our modern system of justice.

✎ Quick Check

1. *What was the Justinian Code? Why was it important?*

2. *In what ways did Justinian change Constantinople?*

3. *Why did many people complain about Justinian's rule?*

4. *How did Justinian and Theodora put down the rebellion in 532?*

5. *How did Justinian rule strictly but fairly?*

29
The Byzantine Way

Justinian and his armies had conquered a great empire. It encircled almost the entire Mediterranean Sea and included parts of Spain, North Africa, and Egypt. After Justinian's death, some territories were lost, and the empire shrank.

An empire that lasts 1,000 years has many great rulers. Another was Basil II, who took the throne in 976. He was a strong emperor who ruled with an iron hand. Under his rule, Byzantine soldiers pushed north and east. They regained territories in the Middle East and in what is now northern Greece and Bulgaria. This new land made the empire even wealthier and more powerful than it had been before.

The Golden Age of the Empire. During this time, the Byzantines had a cultural golden age. Artists, musicians, and architects were respected and well paid. Education became even more important. Several new universities were built in Constantinople. The greatest Byzantine poets and historians wrote during this period.

The Byzantine Golden Age was a time when many people could relax and enjoy life. Life in cities such as Constantinople had never been so pleasant. Jugglers and musicians played in the streets. People strolled and talked in groups. They played chess in cafes or attended chariot races in the Hippodrome. Public baths were popular meeting places. Women could only go to the baths at certain hours in the evening. But they could walk in the streets without fear because oil lamps lighted their way.

Yet during this time, there were also

threats to the empire's survival. Western Europeans, Slavic peoples from Russia and Eastern Europe, and Muslim peoples in Asia wanted a piece of Byzantine wealth and territory. The Byzantines were forced to defend their empire many times. They did so in different ways. Some men fought in the army. Others believed that they served the empire's best interests by devoting their lives to God.

The time: 1024.

The place: a home in Constantinople.

The scene: a man, Phobas (FOH-bahs), is talking to his 14-year-old grandsons, Jason and John. Jason wants to become a special kind of soldier called a *cataphract* (KAT-uh-frakt). Cataphracts are mounted soldiers. They and their horses wear heavy armor. His cousin John wants to become a monk. Monks are members of religious groups. They usually live apart from the world, in small, closed communities called monasteries (MAHN-uh-stair-eez).

PHOBAS: So you boys think you know what you want to do with your lives?

JOHN: Yes, Grandfather. I want to serve God by becoming a monk.

JASON: I want to serve God's agent, the emperor. I want to help defend the empire against its enemies.

PHOBAS: Those are both noble ambitions. But you have not chosen easy paths. Monks and soldiers face many difficulties.

JOHN: That is true. But God will give us strength. The life of a monk demands

The Grand Lavra, largest and richest of the monasteries on Mount Athos, Greece.

many sacrifices. It is through humility and prayer that I will learn God's plan for my life.

JASON: Do you really think you can stand life in a monastery? I, myself, like hearty meals. I don't think I could stand the simple meals that monks eat. And I like to have fun. I wouldn't like to spend most of my time in prayer.

JOHN: Food is just fuel for our bodies. I do not need fancy food. And prayer is a way of being nearer to God. But prayer is only one of the ways a monk spends his time. I would hope to be a part of a monastery that helps people. Perhaps I would help to care for the sick. Or perhaps I would be a scholar.

PHOBAS: Have you thought of becoming a missionary? You know that our church sent teachers to the Slavs. Why, two of our monks even made up an alphabet for the Slavs to use. Many other people have yet to hear about Christ and the Gospel. You could carry the word of God to them.

JASON: Spreading the word of God is important. But we need soldiers as well as monks.

PHOBAS: We certainly could not become a great empire without soldiers. The world is full of enemies. Other people envy our many riches. Western Europeans and Muslims, to name a few, would love to capture Constantinople.

JASON: I think soldiers lead a glorious life. And the cataphracts are the finest soldiers in the world.

PHOBAS: The cataphracts are good soldiers, it is true. But it is not bravery alone that lets them win battles. They often have a little help from our "Greek fire."

JASON: What is that, Grandfather?

PHOBAS: In a battle, our soldiers use copper pipes to spray out a mixture of special chemicals. These burst into flames and can even burn on top of water.

With Greek fire, we are almost unbeatable in a sea battle. Just before I was born, Russia's Prince Igor (EE-gawr) sent 10,000 ships to capture Constantinople. Our navy set fire to all of them. So you see, it is not enough to just have armies. We must have clever people who can invent things to help in our defense.

JOHN: We modern Romans must try to avoid battles if we can. First we must use our money and our brains. Only if other means fail should we use our armies. Armies should not be wasted.

PHOBAS: So you see, Jason, defending the empire requires more than armies. Sometimes we must use spies. Sometimes we must use bribes. At times, our emperor has even paid other armies to go away and leave us alone. Other times, we have made peace with other people by marriage. For example, we have arranged for some of our princesses to marry Russian rulers. At least our women have taught those wild Slavs some manners.

JASON: Is that why we give out so many honors and titles to visitors? To keep their people from bothering us?

PHOBAS: Of course. We tell the visitor that he can be part of our Roman empire. We give him a title. Maybe we give him a fancy robe. He goes home in his fine robe. Everyone admires him. And maybe his people won't attack us.

JASON: I can see that it takes a lot more than armies to defend our empire. But soldiers are still important. I'd rather be a soldier than anything else.

PHOBAS: Well, you seem to know what you want. I'll speak to my friend, the commander.

JASON: Thank you, Grandfather. I'm eager to start my career.

PHOBAS: And you, John, should make a good monk. I know the abbot at the monastery in the hills nearby. Perhaps you would like to visit there. It is never too early to prepare for a religious life.

The Empire Declines. In spite of the surge of Byzantine power under Basil II, the empire was soon in trouble. The decline of the empire began with a battle against Muslim Turks, Asian peoples who ruled lands south and east of the Empire. Byzantine armies were defeated in Asia by the Turks in 1071 at the Battle of Manzikert. As the empire weakened, it began to lose control over the busy trade that had helped to make it rich. Western European merchants competed with Byzantine merchants. Once, the emperor had collected a lot of money from taxes on trade. Now, tax collections shrank. There was less money to pay for the empire's armies.

Quarrels between Roman Catholics and Eastern Orthodox Christians added to the empire's troubles. Catholics wanted to "save" the people of the Byzantine empire by bringing them into the Roman Catholic Church. But most Byzantines had no desire to be "saved."

They clung firmly to their own Christian traditions.

In 1096, Catholics from Western Europe began a series of wars in the Middle East. Those wars were called the Crusades. Their main purpose was to take control of the Holy Land (Jerusalem and surrounding lands) from its Muslim rulers. But on the way, the Crusaders passed through Constantinople. They saw its great riches. Some of the Crusaders wanted those riches for themselves.

Later Crusaders made war against the Byzantines as well as the Muslims. On the Fourth Crusade, in 1204, Crusaders sacked the city of Constantinople. They carried off much of its art and treasure. The Byzantine empire lost many of its lands at this time. Now the empire consisted of little more than Constantinople and a few surrounding territories.

Muslims Invade. Meanwhile, Muslim Turks were gaining strength. A great leader, Osman I, was the first of a powerful line of Turkish rulers. His rule began in 1290 and lasted almost forty years. Later Turkish leaders captured large areas around Constantinople. In 1453, the Turks attacked Constantinople. For two months they tried to break through its walls. Finally their large cannons blasted a hole in the walls.

Turkish soldiers poured through the wall and sacked the city. The leader Mehmed II, took over. This time, the Byzantine empire did not survive. Constan-

Muslim soldiers and sailors surround the walled city of Constantinople before their final, successful attack.

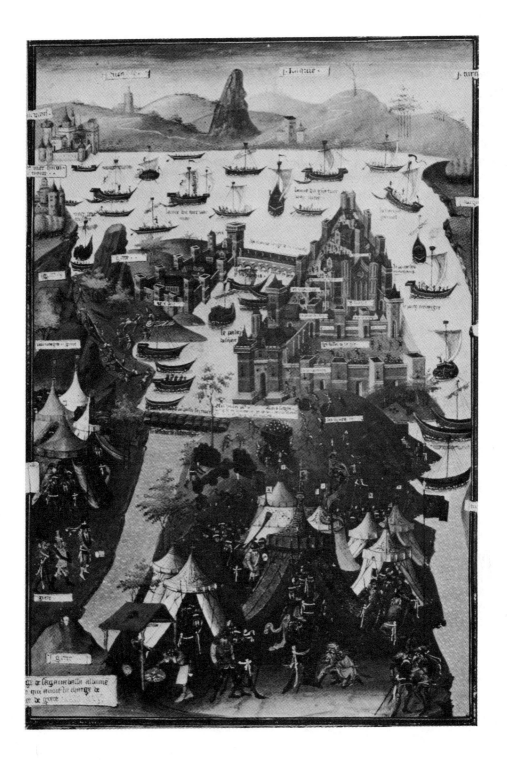

tinople became part of a Muslim empire.

Little is left of the Byzantines' Constantinople. Hagia Sophia, the great church built by Justinian, still stands. But it is now a museum. Yet the Byzantine way of life still lingers in a few Greek villages. And some monasteries preserve many of the rituals and skills of a thousand years ago.

✎ **Quick Check**

1. *What role did monks play in Byzantine life?*

2. *How did a cataphract fight?*

3. *How did the Byzantines try to advance their empire's interests in the world?*

4. *Why were the Crusades a troublesome time for the Byzantines?*

5. *How did the Byzantine empire end?*

THE BYZANTINE EMPIRE

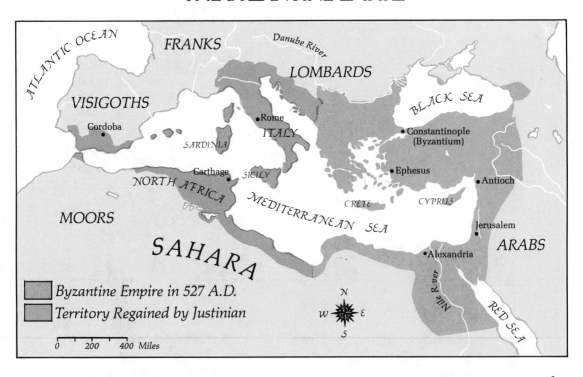

Emperor Justinian ruled from 527 to his death in 565 A.D. Use the map to answer the following questions:

1. The Byzantine empire included lands in three continents. Name all three. Look at the map, page 214, if you need help.

2. True or false? Justinian controlled most of the Mediterranean?

30
Out of Arabia: The Bedouins

In the seventh century, new armies swept out of the deserts of southwest Asia. Those armies were made up of people called Arabs. They conquered Persia and took huge chunks of land from the Byzantines. In the eighth century, their empire spread across North Africa into Spain. It spread deeper into Asia. The Arabs controlled more land than Rome had in its days of greatest power.

People of the Desert. The Arabs were people who came from the Arabian Peninsula. They spoke the Arabic language and lived the Arabic way of life. Most Arabs also shared the religion of Islam.

But before we look at Islam, let's look at the people of the desert where Islam was born.

Today the Arabian desert is as it was 14 centuries ago—hot, dry, and barren. Only the tough survive. A proud people lived there: the Bedouins (BEHD-uh-

winz). The word means "people who live and move in the desert."

For hundreds of years, there have been Bedouin peoples in Arabia. Their values and ways of thinking still help shape the Arab world today. Some of those values have existed for centuries. To get a better idea of them, let's look back at the Arabian desert in the sixth century, before Islam began.

A group of Bedouins is about to move. People are packing up special stones that have been kept in a small red tent. The stones represent deities that are sacred to the group. They believe that the spirits of the deities live in the stones. The stones are the group's idols. Wherever the group goes, the idols go too.

Women are taking down tents made of goatskin and camelskin. Other women are rolling up rugs. Men are rounding up the camels, goats, and horses. It's time to move to a place where wells can be dug. When the wells run dry, the group will move again. Wherever the people go, they take their tents and their herds of animals.

Hassan (hah-SAHN), a handsome fellow in white robes, is watching the work. He is chanting a poem. People listen and smile. They think that Hassan's words are as smooth as honey. He is the community's poet, and his role is an honored one. Other members of the group make poems, but his are the best.

Hassan is also a fine rider. He's a good shot with the bow and arrow. But Hassan's greatest gift is his way with the Arabic language. His poems are important. Poems can be carried in a person's head as the group moves from place to place.

Men gather to listen to Hassan's poems. But the women keep working. They keep their eyes to the ground. Later, the women can talk among themselves. They, too, will make poems and songs. But when men are about, the women keep a respectful silence.

Today, Hassan's first poem is an old favorite. It jokes about the members of another group. It says their men are cowards and their horses are knock-kneed. As Hassan chants the poem, his people laugh.

Now Hassan's voice changes. His next poem tells of a blood feud. A man from another community has killed someone from Hassan's group. The group must take revenge on the killer. An eye for an

eye is the rule of the Bedouin.

The listeners grow angrier with each line of the poem. Some of them remember that the story Hassan is telling happened 20 years ago. Hassan is the group's memory. His poems are the community's history, its music, its newspaper.

Now Hassan chants a terrible story. A Bedouin has committed the greatest crime of all: He has been untrue to his group. He has betrayed a *sheik* (sheek), or local leader. The shame is more than the listeners can bear. They hang their heads and mutter angrily.

But now the tone changes again. Hassan chants a beautiful poem about a traveler who visits the group. It tells of the fruit and the camel's milk the stranger will be offered. The poem says that the guest will be safe in the group's tents. The group will guard him when he rides away. He is a stranger, but he is welcome. It is the rule of the desert. Who knows when someone in Hassan's group will be a stranger traveling in the burning sands?

It is time to move on. Hassan's people have been here long enough.

As they leave their campground, the men will ride guard. There are many raiding parties in the desert. There are many feuds among desert peoples. It is especially important to protect the women of the group.

Hassan's group raids mostly villages. His people look down on villagers and their ways. What kind of people grow

Besides transportation, camels were almost the only source of milk, cheese, wool, and leather for desert peoples.

crops for a living? What life is that for a free person? Even women have more freedom in the desert.

But scorn for the villagers is mixed with a touch of envy. Some villages have grown into towns. They lie on trade routes, where caravans go back and forth. Merchants in the villages are sometimes very rich. They get spices from southern Arabia, silks from China, ivory from Africa. Sometimes Bedouins organize raiding parties to get some of these riches for themselves.

Now the camels are loaded and ready to move. The sheik looks back, then signals his people on. He is important, but still just a man among equals. The men of his group have chosen him because he is wise and brave. He has more wives and more camels than most. And he is proudest of his second son, Hassan, the group's poet and best fighter.

✎ Quick Check

1. *What were the religious beliefs of the Bedouins in the sixth century?*

2. *How did the life of the Bedouins differ from the life of Arabs in villages and towns?*

3. *How did the lives of women in Hassan's community differ from the lives of men?*

4. *Why were poems important to the Bedouins?*

5. *What do the Bedouin poems tell you of their values?*

31
Muhammad:
The Great Prophet

In the seventh century a new religion came to the desert that Hassan called home. The religion was called Islam, meaning "surrender to God." Those who accepted the new religion—who agreed to surrender to God—were called Muslims.

Islam began with a man named Muhammad (muh-HAH-mahd). At first, his followers were few. But within a few years Muhammad's teachings began to spread like wildfire. Today Islam has followers in much of Africa and Asia, and in many other parts of the world. It is the religion of about 550 million people.

Who was Muhammad? What was his message? Why did Islam win over so many people? As it happens, we know more about him than we do about most founders of religions. Muhammad's story speaks for itself.

Muhammad's Early Life. It begins in Mecca, a town near the western coast of the Arabian Peninsula. Mecca was on an important trade route. Arab merchants often passed through Mecca. Other Arabs came to Mecca to worship. To them, Mecca was a holy city. Here, one could find idols representing many of the deities worshiped in Arabia. And one could kiss a special black stone that was known far and wide. People said the stone had fallen from heaven in ancient times. Those who kissed the stone hoped to win heaven's blessing.

Muhammad was born in Mecca about the year 570. His father died before he was born. When he was six, his mother died. The boy was an orphan, and a poor one. But his family was part of Mecca's leading group. Relatives looked after him.

When Muhammad grew up, he had to

In a legend about Muhammad's youth, a Christian monk (bowing) recognizes the boy as a prophet. Angel at top anoints Muhammad's head with holy water.

earn his living. He was a shepherd at first. Later he became a camel driver. Many people praised his honesty and gentle nature. They nicknamed him *al-Amin*, which means "trustworthy."

At the age of about 25, Muhammad married a rich widow named Khadija (kah-DEE-juh). They had four daughters together. For 15 or 20 years, Muhammad led a quiet life. Because he no longer worried about earning a living, he had time to think about religion.

Muhammad looked around him and saw that rich people ignored the prob-lems of the poor. In Mecca and on his travels, he learned about Jewish and Christian ideas. He gave them deep thought. He was very interested in the idea of having only one deity instead of many. This idea is called *monotheism* (mahn-uh-THEE-ihz-ahm).

A Vision in the Desert. Like other Ar-abs, Muhammad would often go into the desert to think. When he was about 40, he believed an angel spoke to him in a desert cave. The voice told him that he must become God's messenger. He was to pass on God's word to all people.

197

Abu Bakr protects Muhammad from being stoned by an angry mob in Mecca (left). Holy man teaches a prince about the ways of Allah (right).

Several more times Muhammad had these dreams or visits. Then he began to preach his new ideas. He told people that there was only one god, who was called Allah (AHL-uh). He was the creator of all people. He wanted the rich to help the poor. Muhammad also warned that a day of judgment was coming. At that time, Allah would separate the believers from the unbelievers. The believers would go to heaven, which was a paradise. The unbelievers would suffer pain in hell.

For several years Muhammad preached. But he won few followers.

Only a handful of people accepted Muhammad as a true prophet—Allah's messenger. Still, some of Mecca's leaders worried. The town made a lot of money from people who visited its holy places. Would Mecca lose money if Muhammad's ideas caught on?

It was dangerous for Muhammad to stay in Mecca. One night in 622, he and a few friends slipped away. They went north to another town. There, the people welcomed him and his followers. They renamed their town in his honor, calling it Medina (muh-DEE-nuh), which means

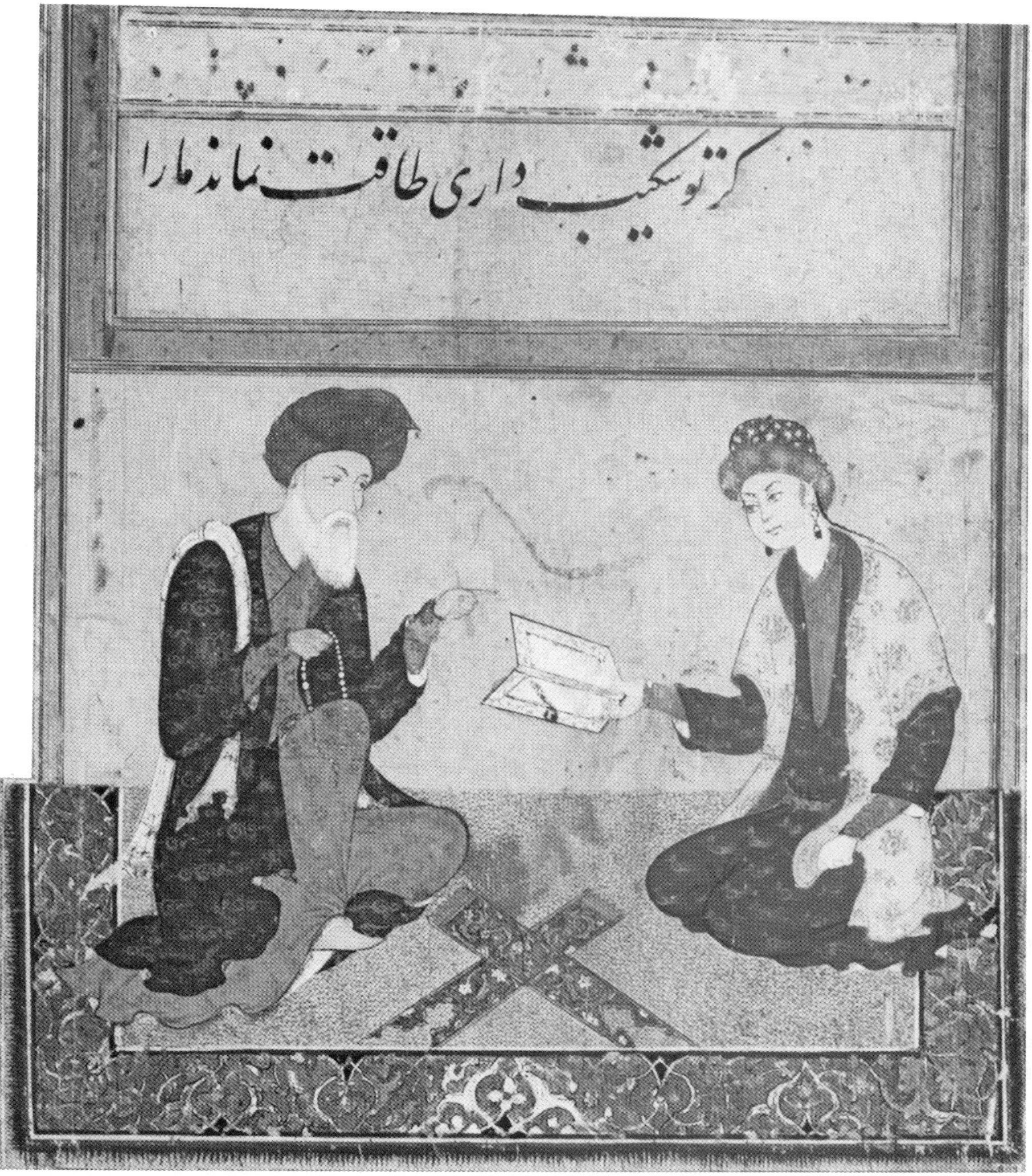
گر تو شکیب داری طاقت نماند ما را

"the city of the prophet." Muslims start their calendar with the year of Muhammad's flight to Medina. It is their year one.

Muhammad's Teachings. In Medina, Muhammad won many new followers. He told of new messsages from Allah. His followers wrote down what the said. The writings were later collected in a book called the Koran (kuh-RAHN). The Koran is the holy book of Islam. Muslims believe it contains the direct words of Allah, as passed on by Muhammad.

Muhammad taught that all people who accepted Islam were part of one family. That message had a powerful impact. Formerly, Arabs had been deeply divided. They had been loyal to their own small groups or communities. Those who accepted Islam now had a higher cause. They discovered a unity that had never existed before.

Islam Spreads. Muhammad became more than a religious leader. He also became a ruler and warrior. At first his rule was limited to Medina. Then it expanded. In 630 Muhammad led an army against Mecca and captured it. He destroyed the idols. He honored the famous black stone and made it part of the Islamic faith.

From his bases in Medina and Mecca, Muhammad set out to unify the peoples of Arabia. Muslim armies pushed to the north. Riding on magnificent Arabian horses, the Muslims galloped out of the desert. They struck fast. Then they disappeared back into the desert.

By 632 Muhammad and his followers had won many victories. Their empire was growing. Muhammad's followers believed they were creating a state governed by the will of Allah. Then, suddenly, Muhammad died. Many of his followers panicked. They had thought he could not die.

But his friend Abu Bakr (ah-BOO BACK-ur) calmed them. He said: "If you are worshipers of Muhammad, know that Muhammad is dead. If you are worshipers of Allah, know that Allah is alive and does not die."

Then Abu Bakr quoted the words of Muhammad: "Muhammad is a prophet only. There have been prophets before him. If he dies or is killed, will you turn back?"

The Muslims did not turn back. They believed that Allah wanted them to spread the faith of Islam. They carried their religion to Africa, Asia, and Europe. Millions of people became Muslims in the next few centuries.

✎ Quick Check

1. *How does the name "Islam" describe the beliefs of Muslims?*

2. *Why did some people in Mecca dislike Muhammad's teachings?*

3. *Why do Muslims consider the Koran to be a holy book?*

4. *How did Muhammad's teachings and actions help to unify the Arabs?*

5. *What main similarity is there between Islam and the older religions of Judaism and Christianity?*

THE ARABIAN PENINSULA: RAINFALL MAP

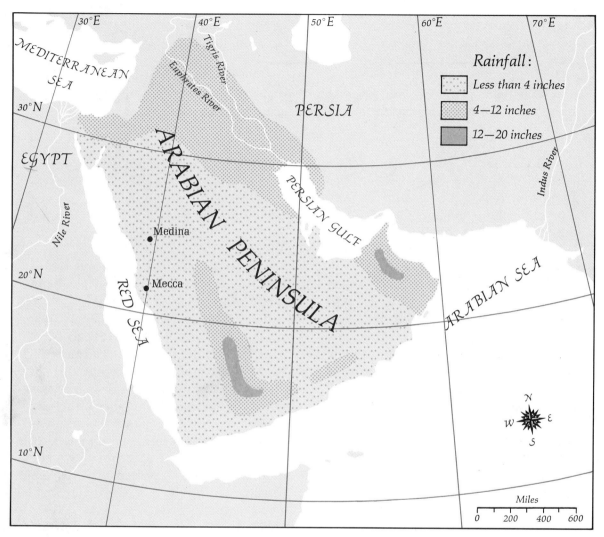

A rainfall map of the Arabian Peninsula can help answer many questions about the area. Use the map to answer the following questions:

1. What important item that people and animals need is in short supply in most of Arabia? How does that explain why Bedouin Arabs move around so much?

2. One definition for a desert is "a region with fewer than 10 inches of rainfall a year." Does most of Arabia fit that definition?

3. Do you think Arabia can support a large population? Explain.

32
The Spread of Islam

Muhammad's friend Abu Bakr became the first *caliph* (KAY-luhf) of the Muslim world. The word caliph means "one who comes after the prophet of Allah." The caliph was part religious leader, part government chief.

Conquering Warriors. Under Abu Bakr and later caliphs, Muslim armies won many battles. They took much land from the Byzantines and conquered the Persian empire. These two peoples were worn out from fighting each other. They were no match for the Arabs. Muslim armies swept west across North Africa as far as the Atlantic Ocean.

Muhammad had urged Muslims to fight for their faith. The Koran says that a person who dies fighting for Islam will go straight to paradise. Often, though, Arab fighters were able to win victories without much bloodshed. Many of the people they conquered didn't mind having the Arabs take over. One reason was that the Arabs often set lower taxes than the old rulers had.

As the Arab empire grew, Muslims tried to win people peacefully to Islam. Muslims did not force the Christians and Jews they conquered to accept the new faith. But there were benefits for those who did. Muslims sometimes paid lower taxes than other people. People who switched to Islam had a better chance of keeping their land. Many of the conquered people decided to become Muslims.

The time: 660.
The place: a village in Syria.
The scene: Arab armies have beaten the Byzantines in this region. Muslims have taken over. Abdul, an Arab Muslim, is trying to get people to accept Islam. He is talking to a Christian named Philip and a Jew named Joseph.

ABDUL: We Muslims have great respect for your faiths. Like the Jews, we honor Abraham and Moses. Like the Christians, we honor Jesus. All three were great prophets. But they did not set forth the complete message of Allah. Only Muhammad, the last and greatest prophet, did that.

JOSEPH: You see Muhammad, then, as a kind of god?

ABDUL: Oh, not at all. There is no god but Allah. Muhammad was Allah's messenger, but Muhammad was not a god.

PHILIP: Then do you look upon Muhammad as the son of Allah? That is how we Christians look upon Jesus.

ABDUL: No, Muhammad was not a son of Allah. He was a man, like you and me. But he was a very important man. We believe that Allah chose Muhammad to be his voice on earth.

JOSEPH: What happens if I refuse to convert to Islam? If I stay a Jew?

ABDUL: Your choice will be respected. The Koran says we must protect Jews and Christians. We all believe in the same God. But only Muslims follow the Koran and worship God, or Allah, in the one true way. So you will not go to paradise when you die. You will suffer. And on this earth you will pay high taxes.

JOSEPH: That's the catch, isn't it? Either become a Muslim or pay up.

ABDUL: It is for your own good. For your soul…Listen. There is the call to worship. Please excuse me. I must stop for prayer. (*Abdul turns toward Mecca. He kneels to pray. All around, other Muslims are doing the same. While Abdul is praying, Joseph and Philip talk quietly.*)

JOSEPH: I will never change my religion. It is the faith of my father, and of his father before him.

PHILIP: My family has been Christian for many generations. I too would never change.

JOSEPH: Still, I think we are better off now than we were before. The Byzantines made us pay such heavy taxes!

PHILIP: And they had their own ideas about Christianity. Imagine—we Syrians were among the very first Christians. Yet those Byzantines tried to tell us what to believe!

JOSEPH: Have you noticed? Some of what the Muslims believe is similar to what we Jews believe. That there is one God. That Abraham and Moses were prophets. And Muslims, like Jews, must not eat pork.

PHILIP: Yes, but much is different too. These people use neither liquor nor wine. Alcohol is forbidden to Muslims. Yet both Jews and Christians use wine in their rituals.

JOSEPH: There seem to be both similiarities and differences among our three religions.

ABDUL (*rising from prayer*): I'm sorry to have interrupted our talk. I wanted to tell you more about our beliefs.

JOSEPH: Please go on.

ABDUL: Our faith is set down in Allah's Holy Book, the Koran. There are five great rules. I have told you the first: "There is no god but Allah, and Muhammad is His Prophet." The second rule is to pray five times a day. When we hear the call to prayer, we stop whatever we are doing. We face Mecca and pray.

PHILIP: And the other rules?

ABDUL: One must treat all Muslims as brothers and sisters and give alms to the poor. That's three. Do not eat between sunrise and sunset in the holy month of Ramadan (RAH-mah-dan). That's four. The fifth rule is that you must visit Mecca once in your life if you can.

JOSEPH: That seems simple. Is that all?

ABDUL: Those rules may seem simple, but

THE MUSLIM EMPIRE

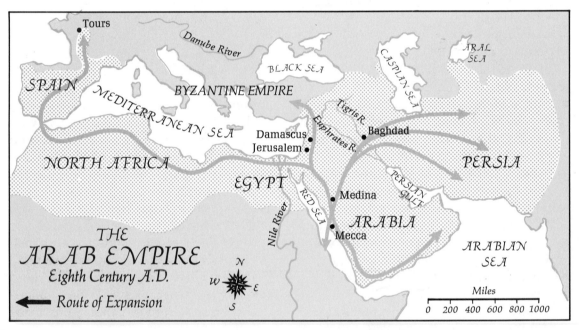

As the Muslim empire grew, Muslims spread the faith of Islam. Use the map to answer the following questions:

1. The Muslim empire included lands on three continents. What were these continents? Use the map, page 214, if you need help.

2. What European nation was probably most influenced by the Muslims?

3. Describe the route of the Muslim soldiers from Medina to Tours.

they are not. They fit into a whole way of life. The Koran sets down laws about every part of life. It tells how one should live in one's family. And in one's community. And in one's nation. A true Muslim must follow the will of Allah in everything he does.

PHILIP: Tell me about the family. Some Muslim men I know have several wives. Is that also a part of your religion?

ABDUL: Yes. The Koran says a man may have as many as four wives at once. As a matter of fact, I have three wives myself.

JOSEPH: How do you keep them from leaving you? Don't they mind sharing one husband?

ABDUL: I treat my wives kindly. I protect them from all harm. The Koran tells us to do so. It says that wives have a duty to respect their husbands. But it also says that wives have rights that we must respect. For example, our wives can own their own property.

PHILIP: I hear that your faith also tells you how to treat your slaves.

ABDUL: Yes. Muhammad wanted us to treat our slaves as human beings. They are allowed to get married. If they want, they can save up money to buy their freedom. The Koran encourages us to free our slaves whenever we can. Also, no Muslim can enslave another Muslim. If a person becomes a Muslim, they are freed.

JOSEPH: Doesn't it take a long time to become a Muslim? To become a Jew, one must study for a long time.

ABDUL: It is much simpler with us. We have no priests. No one lets you into the faith. You must enter by yourself. To become a Muslim, all you need to do is say that you accept the faith. You surrender to Allah. That's all. You are then a Muslim. You follow the rules. But once you are a Muslim, you cannot go back. Otherwise you will suffer in hell.

Not all the people the Arabs conquered accepted the Muslim faith. But many of them did. By the middle of the eighth century, the Muslims had taken much of North Africa and had moved into Spain. They had won new followers for their religion everywhere they went.

The Muslims might even have won over Western Europe if it hadn't been for one event. They were defeated by a European army in a battle near Tours, France, in 732. As a result of that battle, Muslim armies were driven back. They did not push north from Spain again.

✎ Quick Check

1. *Why did some conquered people welcome the Arab Muslims?*

2. *Why did Muslims have a special regard for Jews and Christians?*

3. *Did Muslims worship Muhammad? Explain.*

4. *What are the five great rules of Islam?*

5. *What might a Muslim woman of the seventh century have liked about her place in society? What might she have disliked?*

33
The Age of the Caliphs

Like people everywhere, Muslims argued about religion and politics. They often disagreed about who should be caliph. And they disagreed on what the duties of the caliph should be. At first, the caliphs were mostly concerned with war and expanding the Muslim empire. They were good military leaders. Under their rule, Muslim territory greatly increased (see map page 204). These rulers were called the Umayyad (oo-MEE-yad) caliphs.

Revolt in the Empire. Unfortunately, many people were unhappy with the Umayyad caliphs. One of the reasons was that they made laws that treated non-Arab Muslims like second-class citizens. These laws went against the ideas of Muhammad. Muhammad had taught that all Muslims should be treated the same way, regardless of race.

In 750, Arabs and non-Arabs throughout the Muslim empire revolted against the Umayyad caliphs. New caliphs called the Abbasids (AB-ah-sihdz) came to power. The Abbasids ruled all of the empire except Spain, which kept its Umayyad leader.

The Abbasids ruled from the city of Baghdad. That city is now the capital of Iraq. It was one of the grandest cities in all the world.

Baghdad was the most important center of culture for the Abbasids. Muslim conquerors had learned much from the people they defeated. By the time of the Abbasids, education had become very important. One in five people in the em-

pire could read, which was a great many at that time in history. Muslim scholars from Baghdad led the world in some fields. Among these were mathematics, medicine, and astronomy. And Baghdad's library housed thousands of books.

Let's imagine a visit to Baghdad in its days of glory. It is the year 890. A man stands near the city center. He is giving directions to two young students.

Oh, so you are travelers. Well, travelers come here every day. Some come for business. Some come to study. The Round City of Baghdad has something for everyone...

Why do we call it the Round City? You can see for yourselves. The thick walls form a circle. They go around the city center. Of course, we have spilled out past the walls now. Seventy years have come and gone since the caliph al-Mansur (ahl mahn-SOOR) had the walls built. Baghdad is at the crossroads of the world. Caravans pass through from near and far. How quickly the city has grown!

You say you are students. You, young fellow, sound like an Egyptian. Am I right?...You say you are studying the stars? Well, you've come to the right place. Our astronomers are famous all over the world. Their workplace is not far down that street.

And you, young man? You look like you come from the land of the Franks. Europe, is it called? You say you are looking for the House of Wisdom. What a center of learning it is! Wait till you see the great library.

Are you looking for a job? I can tell that you speak Arabic well. Do you also know Greek or Persian? The caliph is having the classics of every great language put into Arabic. There is work for many scholars. We must translate the books into our own language. We use other people's knowledge. Then we add on to it.

Will you study under one of our teachers?...Oh, you are learning medicine. Then you have come to the right city. Our doctors are writing books about diseases that no one has understood before. Diseases with names such as smallpox and measles. They are finding cures for diseases of the eye. They are doing new operations that you would not believe!

Please stop and visit our free public hospital. Even the poor need the help of doctors. Allah is great. Allah wills that we help the poor.

You say you had not expected such a large and modern city? Well, I do hate to brag, but everything here is very up-to-date. Have you any idea how many artisans worked to make Baghdad beautiful?

Muslims remained leaders in the field of astronomy. Here, astronomers use sixteenth-century instruments to measure distances on land and sea.

Folk art decorates an early recipe for cough medicine.
Muslim doctors were pioneers in the field of medicine.

Is it possible to see the caliph? Well, no. The Commander of the Faithful is not seen by ordinary people. His bodyguards keep him apart.

Excuse me. There is the call to prayer. I must go.

The Empire Splits. The rule of the Abbasids lasted until 1055. But they were unable to keep Muslim territory united even during their rule. A new group of caliphs, the Fatimids (FAT-ih-midz), came to power in northern Africa. In 1055, the

210

great Muslim empire was split in three parts.

The Abbasid caliphs lost control of Baghdad in 1055. But the conquerors were not other Arabs. They were Muslim Turks, Asian peoples from the deserts north and east of Baghdad. For almost 100 years they had lived as subjects of the caliph. They had become Muslims. They had given slaves and soldiers to help the Arab caliphs rule. Now they felt it was their turn to rule the Muslim empire.

At this time, the Turks were led by a family called Seljuk (SEHL-jook). Seljuk leaders were called sultans (SUHLT-uhnz). After conquering much of the old Muslim empire, they created a large empire of their own. The caliph in Baghdad had only religious duties now. He was no longer a great ruler. But Baghdad still thrived as a center of Muslim culture.

The Muslim religion was still spreading. From Baghdad, Arabs traveled farther and farther east. They moved into parts of India, converting new followers to Islam there. In time Muslims carried their religion to China. Islam was also spread to Southeast Asia. Today the many-island nation of Indonesia has more than 150 million Muslims.

Fall of the Seljuks. Before long, the Seljuk Turks began to weaken. Like the Arabs, they quarreled. Their empire split into several parts. The Seljuks could not defend Baghdad. In 1258 the city fell to still another Asian group, the Mongols (see Chapter 15). The Mongols dumped books from the great library into the Tigris River. They killed the caliph and many others. Some say 800,000 people died. No one knows for sure.

The Mongols were not Muslims. They had no interest in making Baghdad their capital. Trade began to bypass Baghdad and Iraq. New routes passed through Egypt to the west, and through Persia to the east. Baghdad's days of glory were past. But Muslim culture still thrived in other wealthy cities.

In the thirteenth century, a group called the Ottoman Turks grew strong. After 1453 the empire's capital was in Constantinople, the old Byzantine capital. At its height, the Ottoman empire stretched from North Africa to Iraq. It reached from Arabia to Eastern Europe. The Ottoman empire would be the chief Muslim power between the sixteenth and twentieth centuries.

✎ **Quick Check**

1. *Why did Baghdad become an important city?*

2. *In what fields of study did Muslim scholars gain fame?*

3. *How did the Muslim empire help to pass on the learning of earlier times?*

4. *In what major countries of eastern Asia did Islam become important?*

5. *How were the Arabs replaced as leaders of the Muslim empire?*

PART 6
Review and Skills Exercises

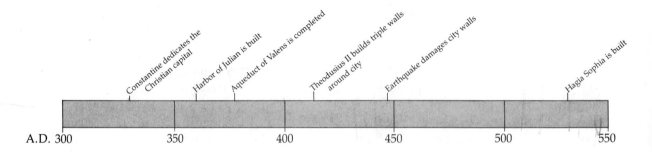

Constantine dedicates the Christian capital

Harbor of Julian is built

Aqueduct of Valens is completed

Theodosius II builds triple walls around city

Earthquake damages city walls

Hagia Sophia is built

A.D. 300   350   400   450   500   550

Understanding Events

As you read in Part 6, Constantinople became the capital of the Byzantine Empire. The time line above lists some of the events that took place in Constantinople during the city's early years. Study the time line and answer the questions that follow.

1. In what century did Constantine have Christian churches built in his new capital?

2. What changes were made to the city during the fourth century?

3. Constantine had walls built along the city's coasts. About how many years passed before more walls were built?

4. What natural disaster is recorded on the time line? When did it happen?

5. How long had the city been the capital by the time Justinian and Theodora had the Hagia Sophia built?

Interpreting a Reading

Read the paragraphs below and answer the questions that follow.

The New Rome

Emperors think in grand terms. The Roman emperor Constantine thought in very grand terms when he moved the capital of the Roman Empire to Byzantium and named it New Rome. Constantine wanted the new capital to be even more magnificent than Rome.

New Rome was divided into 14 districts just as Rome was. New buildings were designed to look like buildings in Rome. Constantine brought many statues and valuable pieces of art from Rome. He ordered religious relics brought from many places in the empire and enshrined in Constantinople. The relics were items such as a piece of wood thought to have come from the cross Jesus Christ was crucified on. Constantine built church after church.

212

Old Byzantium had a hippodrome, an oval stadium for horse and chariot races. Constantine enlarged it to hold 60,000 spectators.

The city had at least 150 private baths and many public ones. Both women and men could go to the public baths, but at different times. Water for the city was brought by waterways called aqueducts from hills around the city to cisterns where it was stored. From there the water was piped to fountains around the city so all could use it. Underground drains were dug to carry away the sewage and waste water.

Constantine, like other leaders of the time, greatly feared invasions. He called for a new wall to be built around the city. The city grew fast and spread beyond Constantine's wall. New walls were built. By the fourteenth century the city had become a fortress. Eventually there were 13 miles of walls. A moat was dug where the city faced land. Behind the moat were three walls, one behind the other. Along the walls were many towers where archers stood guard. On the seaward sides of the city stretched more walls. In places these walls were built out to surround and protect the harbors.

Constantine and the emperors who followed him took care to prepare the city in the event of a siege. Water and food were stored inside the city at all times. The fortress worked for more than 1,000 years. It was not until 1453 that invaders, Muslim Turks, succeeded in taking the city. Constantinople—Constantine's New Rome—became the capital of a new empire, the Ottoman Empire.

1. Why do you think Constantine wanted New Rome to be greater than Rome?

2. What public services did Constantinople provide for its people?

3. What made Constantinople a fortress.

4. What is a siege and why would a city need to prepare for one?

Building Vocabulary

Try your skill at matching the words below with the correct definitions. Write the numbers 1-8 on a sheet of paper. Then write the word by each number that matches the definition.

1. Holy writings of Muslims.

2. Belief that there is one God.

3. City where Muhammad was born.

4. Islamic term for Supreme Being.

5. Religious and governmental leader whose name means "one who comes after the prophet of Allah."

6. Followers of this religion consider themselves to have "surrendered to God."

7. Prophet who founded Islam.

8. City whose name means "the city of the prophet."

Medina	Islam
Mecca	Muhammad
Allah	Koran
caliph	monothesim

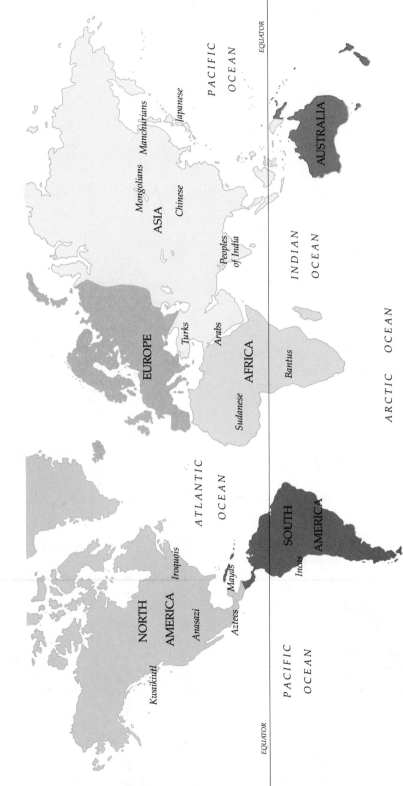

THE WORLD

ARCTIC OCEAN

NORTH AMERICA

Kwaikiutl

Iroquois

Anasazi

Aztecs

Mayas

PACIFIC OCEAN

ATLANTIC OCEAN

SOUTH AMERICA

Incas

EQUATOR

EUROPE

Turks

ASIA

Mongolians

Manchurians

Japanese

Chinese

Peoples of India

Arabs

AFRICA

Sudanese

Bantus

INDIAN OCEAN

PACIFIC OCEAN

EQUATOR

AUSTRALIA

GLOSSARY

adobe. a building material of sun-dried mud and straw.

ahimsa. the Buddhist belief that it is wrong to harm any living creature.

ancestor worship. the Chinese practice of honoring one's ancestors; the ancestors might then help the living.

anthropologist. a scientist who studies past and present cultures.

archaeologist. a scientist who studies cultures through remains, such as tools, weapons, pottery, buildings, and writings.

aristocracy. the upper class of a society.

artisan. a trained or skilled worker; a craftsworker.

Aryans. group of people who migrated into India from the northwest around 1500 B.C.

astronomy. the study of the stars and the planets.

Aztecs. group of native Americans who created a complex culture in the valley of Mexico.

Bedouins. nomadic people of the desert.

Bhagavad Gita. Hindu religious book written in the form of poetry.

Brahman. highest of the Hindu deities; also a Hindu of the upper class who is usually part of the priesthood.

Buddhism. religion of Asia founded by Siddhārtha Gautama, the Buddha; teaches that a person can be freed from the sufferings of life through self-control and by leading a moral life.

bureaucracy. group of people who run an organization, especially a government.

bushido. code of behavior of samurai warriors in early Japan.

Byzantine empire. the eastern part of the Roman empire that flourished in the Middle East from the fourth through the tenth centuries.

caliph. Muslim title; refers to a person who was both a religious and a political leader.

caste. a social class; part of a caste system in which people are ranked according to their occupation, wealth, family, or some other characteristic.

cataphract. a mounted soldier in the Byzantine army. Both horse and soldier wore heavy armor.

cataract. a large, steep waterfall.

character. a letter, figure, or design used in writing or printing.

citadel. high part of an ancient city, whose buildings usually served as a fortress or stronghold.

clan. a group of related families.

Confucianism. teachings of the Chinese philospher Confucius. Confucius preached purity, sincerity, respect for others, and adherence to proper rituals.

Crusades. wars between Western Europeans and Muslims for control of the Holy Land in the Middle East.

culture. the way of life of a people. A culture includes the tools, food, clothing, customs, values, and religion of a people.

daimyo. a great lord in early Japan.

deity. a god or goddess.

doctrine. an official policy or set of principles.

dynasty. a family that rules a country for many generations.

extinct. something that no longer exists or is no longer active.

filial piety. the respect of children for their parents or grandparents.

golden age. a time of growth in art, literature, education, religion, and science.

Great Wall. immense barrier in northern China that stretched about 1,500 miles. Its purpose was to keep out invaders from the north.

Greek fire. special chemicals sprayed at enemy ships by the Byzantine navy. The chemicals burst into flames.

guru. a religious teacher or guide in the Hindu religion.

heretic. a person who holds beliefs that are different from the accepted beliefs of his or her church.

hieroglyph. a picture, character, or symbol that stands for a word, idea, or sound.

Hinduism. the major religion of India, in which many deities are worshiped and which emphasizes the sacredness of all forms of life.

homage. respect; honor.

idol. an image or other object worshiped as a deity.

Incas. native Americans of Peru who created a vast empire in the Andes mountains during the fifteenth century.

infinity. endlessness; space and/or time without boundaries.

Iroquois. powerful group of native Americans who lived in the woodlands of the Northeast United States.

irrigation. supplying water to farmland usually by the use of ditches.

Islam. a major world religion whose followers believe in Allah as the sole deity and Muhammad as his prophet.

jataka. a story about the Buddha told to help people understand his teachings.

jati. a sub-caste in the caste system; a person is born into a particular jati.

Justinian Code. set of laws drawn up by the emperor Justinian to govern the Byzantine empire; became a model for later laws in Western Europe.

kachinas. spirits that Hopi Indians of the Southwest represent through masks and dolls.

kiva. a room traditionally used for religious purposes by native Americans of the Southwest.

Koran. the holy book of the followers of Islam.

Legalists. followers of a Chinese philosophy that believed in strict laws and forcing people to be good.

longhouse. a large rectangular dwelling in which several native American families might live.

Mandate of Heaven. the belief that Chinese rulers received their right to rule from spiritual forces.

mansa. the title given to the kings of Mali in Africa.

Mauryan empire. ancient empire of India centered on the Ganges River.

Maya. native Americans of Central America and Mexico who developed an advanced civilization of city-states.

meditate. to think quietly.

mesa. a high, flat hill or plateau.

missionary. a person who travels to different lands and tries to convert people there to his or her beliefs.

monarch. a person who rules over a kingdom or empire.

monk. a man who gives up a worldly life for a religious life. Monks often live away from other people in monasteries.

monotheism. religious belief that there is only one god.

monsoon. an annual spring wind occurring in the region of the Indian Ocean. Also, the name given to the three-month rainy season that accompanies these winds.

mosaic. a picture or design made by fixing small pieces of stone, glass, or other materials on to a surface. The material is usually of different colors.

mosque. a Muslim house of worship.

movable type. individual letters or characters that can be arranged to make words in printing.

Muslim. a follower of the religion of Islam.

nirvana. the state in Buddhism in which a person reaches freedom from suffering.

nomad. a person who wanders from place to place.

obsidian. a dark-colored glass that is formed when lava cools.

philosophy. a system of thought for guiding life; the teachings or ideas of a person or a group.

pilgrimage. a journey to a sacred place.

policy of isolation. the attempt of a nation to stop contacts between itself and other nations.

porcelain. a fine, white clay mixture which when hardened, can be made into beautiful dishes and decorative objects.

potlatch. a feast of the native Americans of the Pacific Northwest. Huge amounts of food and gifts are given away at the feast.

Quechua. the language of the Incas of Latin America; it is still spoken in parts of Peru.

queue. a braid of hair that hangs at the back of the head; worn by Chinese men to show loyalty to the emperor.

quipu. a cord with knotted strings. Used by the Incas to keep records.

Ramadan. holy month in the religion of Islam during which Muslims fast.

rasa. one of eight emotions, such as love or wonder, in a Hindu drama.

sachem. a leader among the Iroquois people of the Northeast woodlands.

sage. a very wise person.

samurai. a warrior in Japan who followed the code called bushido and who served a great lord.

seal. a design carved on stone or other material. Used to mark things to show ownership.

seppuku. The ritual of suicide in Japan in which samurai attempted to get back their lost honor.

sheik. an Arab chieftain or head of a clan.

Shinto. traditional religion of Japan, involving the worship of deities representing the different forces of nature.

shogun. a military lord in Japan who ruled in the name of the emperor. Shoguns ruled Japan until 1868.

sipapu. according to Hopi belief, a hole through which humans came to this world from an underworld.

soothsayer. a person who claims that he or she can tell the future.

standard. guideline; accepted model or

example.

stele. a large piece of stone or a pillar with writings or carvings on it.

subcontinent. a land mass that is large, but smaller than a continent.

Sudan. the grassland of Africa just south of the Sahara Desert; a large country of northeast Africa.

sultan. a title for a ruler of a Muslim country.

surplus. an extra amount of something.

Taoism. Chinese philosophy and religion that believes in bringing people's lives into harmony with nature.

totem pole. a log or pole carved with pictures or symbols by native Americans. The logs were set upright in front of buildings.

veda. the Hindu word for "knowledge." The Vedas, or books of knowledge, are among the earliest and most important works of Hinduism.

yin and yang. in Chinese philosophy, the opposites that exist in nature. Yin is the female side and yang the male.

yoga. a system of exercises that are part of Hinduism and are designed to bring people closer to the Hindu deity.

yogi. a person who practices yoga in order to gain control of the body.

INDEX